the wildlife gardener

the wildlife gardener

CREATING A HAVEN FOR BIRDS, BEES AND BUTTERFLIES

Kate Bradbury

First published in Great Britain
in 2013 by
Kyle Books
an imprint of Kyle Cathie Ltd.
67–69 Whitfield Street
London, W1T 4HF
general.enquiries@kylebooks.com
www.kylebooks.com

10 9 8 7 6 5 4 3 2 1

ISBN: 978-0-85783-157-6

Kate Bradbury is hereby identified
as the author of this work in
accordance with Section 77 of
the Copyright, Designs and
Patents Act 1988.

Project Editors: Emma Bastow
and Jenny Wheatley
Design: Ketchup
Photographer: Julie Watson
Copy editor: Polly Boyd
Editorial Assistant: Laura Foster
Production: Lisa Pinnell

A Cataloguing In Publication record
for this title is available from the
British Library.

Colour reproduction by
ALTA London.
Printed and bound in China
by Toppan Printing Co., Ltd.

Dedication
For Nin, Oscar and Louis

Additional Photo Credits
Alamy: Page 17 Florapix, 18 Steffen Hauser/botanikfoto, 28 (left) Theo Moye, (right) blickwinkel, 45 (bottom right) Nurlan Kalchinov, 49 (top left) imagebroker, 55 Natural Visions, 56 Anna Stowe Botanica, 59 (left) FloralImages, (right) Nature Photographers Ltd, 64–65 (top) Jeremy Pardoe, (bottom) Kathy Wright, 66 Tim Gainey, 76 (top) vario images GmbH & Co.KG, (bottom) imagebroker, 77 blickwinkel, 78 Picture Press, 79 (bottom) Bill Coster, 81 (top) T.M.O. Birds, (bottom) Ian Butler, 82 (top) Colin Varndell, (bottom) tbkmedia.de, 83 (left) Nigel Dowsett, 84 (top) Caroline Eastwood, 85 (top) Gary Tack, 86 (top) imagebroker, (bottom) All Canada Photos, 87 (top) Juniors Bildarchiv GmbH, 90 (top) The Wildlife Studio, (bottom) Naturfoto-Online, 92 (top) Juniors Bildarchiv GmbH, (middle) Kevin Sawford, 94 (top) imagebroker, 95 (top) Chris George, (bottom) David Cole, 100 (top) blickwinkel, 105 (bottom right) Naturepix, 107 (top left) Andrew Darrington, (bottom right) Richard Becker, 108 Malcolm McMillan, 112 (right) Richard Becker, 114 (top) Avico Ltd, 116 (right) FLPA, 118 (top) Neil Hardwick, (bottom) Naturepix, 124 (top left) David Chapman, (top right) imagebroker, (bottom) blickwinkel, 125 (right) David Chapman, 127 (top) Christian Musat, (bottom) Naturepix, 128 (top) WoodyStock, (bottom) Naturepix, 129 (top left) Danita Delimont, (bottom) Custom Life Science Images, 134 (top) FLPA, (bottom right) David Forster, 135 (top left) blickwinkel, (bottom) Andrew Darrington, 138 (bottom) Kasia Nowak **GAP:** 83 (right) Tim Gainey **The Garden Collection:** 68 Marcus Harper (Owner/designer: Stephanie Harrod), 94 (bottom) John Watkins/FLPA **rspb-images.com:** 79 (top) Steve Round.

Contents

Introduction

The wild world on your doorstep

Imagine a world in which blades of grass tower above you. Where trees are giants and flowers big plates of food. In this world you dance to reveal the location of nectar, or deter predators by rolling into a ball. You might be completely harmless but wear the colours of a more sinister animal, or perhaps you started life swimming in a pool which you now only return to once a year, to make babies of your own. Whatever you are and however you live, all you have to do is eat and not be eaten, to mate and not be cuckolded.

This world exists in our gardens. While we're tucked up in the safety and comfort of our homes, tiny beings are hiding in our lawns and eating, mating or even sleeping on our flowers. For some of them an ornamental border is their entire universe; for others our gardens form part of a much larger habitat, spanning whole neighbourhoods and even oceans and continents.

The wonderful thing about gardens is that none of them is devoid of wildlife – every one has insects, birds or the odd mammal passing through. But actively creating homes for wildlife, where hundreds of species can feed, drink and take shelter, is another thing altogether.

By encouraging wildlife to the garden we can help protect local species, connect with nature and learn more about the fascinating wild world on our doorstep. We benefit from natural pest control, improved pollination and healthier soil (and therefore plants). And it's fun; when it's wet we can sit at home and watch frogs hop about on the patio, and when it's cold we can enjoy the antics of birds squabbling over food.

But there's another reason why we garden for wildlife, and perhaps it's the most important. It's the feeling we get when we watch a baby blue tit visit the feeder for the first time, or when we find a lethargic bumblebee on the ground and revive her with a little drop of sugar water. We humans have evolved with animals. Observing and caring for them may have helped shape our language and culture. Caring for wildlife is therefore part of who we are; it's in our bones. Put simply, it's love.

LEFT *Blue-tailed damselflies make a heart-shaped mating wheel.*
OPPOSITE *This long grass provides a habitat for a myriad of creatures.*

millipedes, slugs and thousands of worms breaking down the waste and returning it to the earth. Take a closer look at your plants and you might see the tiny larvae of lacewings, hoverflies and ladybirds making a meal of a cluster of aphids.

You'll also find them in this book, rubbing shoulders with the birds, bees and butterflies, just as they do in our gardens. In the first half I suggest general ways to create garden habitats for wildlife including the provision of shelter, food and water, and in the second part I introduce some of the species we're likely to come across and explain the intricate roles they play.

This book isn't a call to arms to Save the Aphid or Love the Woodlouse, but I hope it will explain the importance of these and other creatures we gardeners have been conditioned to think of unfavourably. And, while this goes against advice in so many gardening books, I'd like us to cherish the aphid, and the woodlouse, caterpillar and crane fly. Just a little. Just enough to keep that world outside our back door turning.

My garden is a tiny bit of land sandwiched between a purpose-built block of flats and a busy cycle path, surrounded by concrete. When I moved here it was a paved courtyard, and my first job was to lift the slabs, buy a tonne of topsoil and scrounge plants from my mum. Along the way I rescued seven baby frogs from a kitchen drain, which were sheltering there after the pond they were spawned in was filled in; I've been dive-bombed by a feisty blackbird who I named Sid, who claimed the garden as his own and bullied the other birds away; and I've watched a brand-new speckled wood butterfly pump its wings in the sunshine. My garden still has a long way to go, but after only three years it already supports a wide range of species, including the blue tits and great tits that raid the borders for caterpillars in spring, a chattering 'charm' of goldfinches and, of course, scores of bees and butterflies.

Our gardens are magical places in which everything is connected and all but the most alien of invaders have a vital role to play. Open your compost bin and you'll find woodlice,

OPPOSITE *Herbaceous borders provide shelter and food for anything from tiny millipedes to amphibians and hedgehogs.* **ABOVE** *A few choice plants like this viper's bugloss can make all the difference to bees.*
ABOVE RIGHT *To garden for toads is to garden for their food, including slugs, snails, ants, beetles and spiders.*

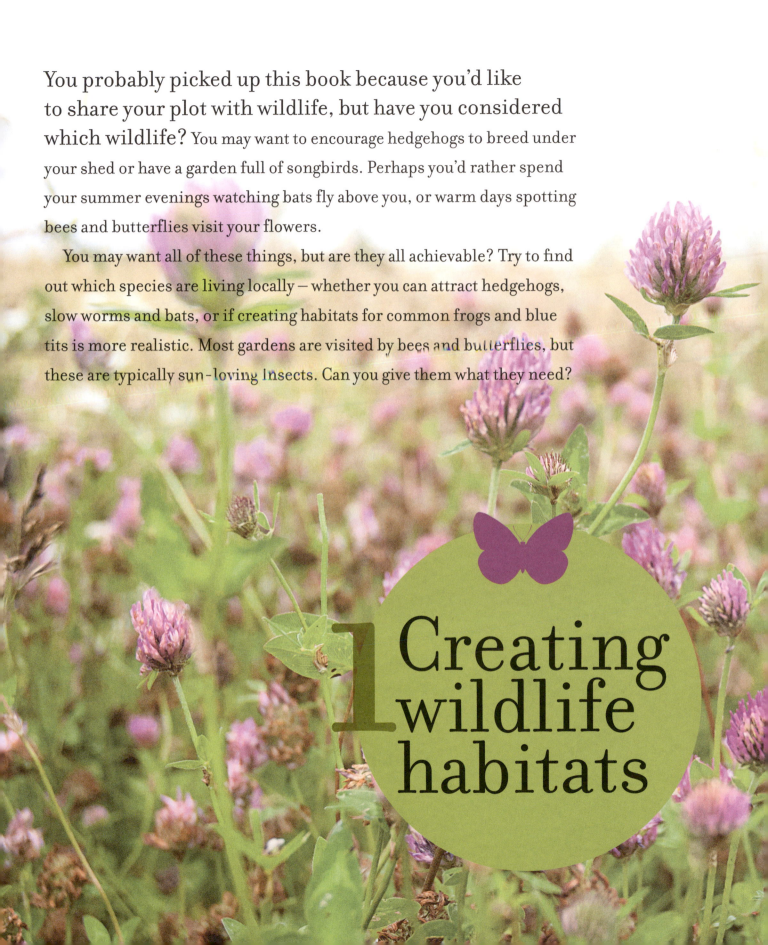

You probably picked up this book because you'd like to share your plot with wildlife, but have you considered which wildlife? You may want to encourage hedgehogs to breed under your shed or have a garden full of songbirds. Perhaps you'd rather spend your summer evenings watching bats fly above you, or warm days spotting bees and butterflies visit your flowers.

You may want all of these things, but are they all achievable? Try to find out which species are living locally — whether you can attract hedgehogs, slow worms and bats, or if creating habitats for common frogs and blue tits is more realistic. Most gardens are visited by bees and butterflies, but these are typically sun-loving insects. Can you give them what they need?

1 Creating wildlife habitats

Choosing your habitats

No matter how big or small your garden, you can create a variety of habitats for wildlife. Even small steps, such as growing a greater selection of flowering plants or composting your garden waste, can make a difference.

In creating habitats you're providing wildlife with shelter, food or water, or a combination of the three. One habitat may not meet every need of one animal, but it can fulfil some needs of many. For example, a pond provides a safe breeding area for frogs, toads, newts, dragonflies and damselflies, and drinking water for birds and hedgehogs. Large ponds may provide a hunting ground for grass snakes or even attract the Daubenton's bat, which has evolved large, hairy feet for the task of scooping insects off the water's surface.

Outside the breeding season, common frogs spend the majority of their lives on land, sheltering in damp, secluded spots such as a log pile. They might eat other inhabitants of the log pile as well as take shelter, so this habitat meets more than one of their needs. A log pile may also make a good habitat for wood-boring beetles, wood mice and wrens – all for different reasons.

So, if you like frogs (or just want them to polish off your slugs and snails), it's a good idea to make a pond, but it's also worth providing habitats for them on land. And if frogs aren't high on your list of species to attract, digging a pond might still be a sensible option if you want to cater for a wide range of other wildlife, including dragonflies.

Creating one habitat provides a piece of the jigsaw puzzle of needs for a great number of species. We can fit the pieces together to create a mosaic of habitats within our gardens or team up with our neighbours to spread it over a wider area. You simply need to establish which species you're most interested in attracting and adjust your garden accordingly.

ABOVE *A densely planted border of nectar-rich plants such as these globe thistles, provides food for pollinators as well as shade and shelter for other species including birds, amphibians and hedgehogs.*

It's no sacrifice

You don't need to dedicate your whole garden to wildlife, grub up your prized cactus dahlias or stop gardening altogether. You can do as much or as little as you would like to. Gardening for wildlife can involve as little as allowing a strip of grass to grow long, or planting a particular type of tree or a small hedge. Maybe you just want to grow the best plants for pollinators. It's your garden; it's up to you.

BELOW *Simply by planting a wider variety of nectar-rich plants, we can encourage more butterflies, like this gatekeeper, to visit.* **ABOVE RIGHT** *The bottom panel of this fence has been removed, allowing frogs and other wildlife to travel easily between gardens.*

Wildlife corridors

It may seem obvious, but if you want to encourage wildlife to your garden the first thing you need to do is physically open it and make it accessible. You might see your plot as an individual, closed space, but many wild species see it as just one part of a much larger habitat, which not only includes your next-door neighbour's plot but could also include the gardens in the adjacent street. Birds, bees and butterflies should easily access your garden, but what about animals that walk, crawl, slither or hop? Look around and ask yourself, 'How will frogs find my pond; how will hedgehogs access my borders?'

Providing a way in (and out) essentially increases the availability of food and shelter to garden wildlife. A hole under a fence is normally all that's needed – simply dig one on either side. You can also remove the lowest slat of a fence panel. Walls are more tricky, but it's not impossible to knock out a brick or two without damaging the structure. If you're worried your dog might run amok in neighbouring gardens, just make sure the hole is smaller than the dog – reinforce it if necessary. Hedgehogs need only 12–15cm to squeeze through. Talking of neighbours, why not encourage them to make holes beneath their boundaries, too? A whole street of linked gardens means your local hedgehogs need never see a car again.

Shelter

ABOVE *Trees and shrubs provide the perfect cover for garden birds, as well as shelter for their insect food.* **OPPOSITE, CLOCKWISE FROM TOP LEFT** *A hedge shelters a dunnock from predators. A hoverfly takes a rest on a leaf. A common lizard makes a getaway to the shelter of undergrowth. A common darter dragonfly and red admiral butterfly bask on a wooden post.*

I once spotted a queen bumblebee squeeze herself into my willow garden fence a second before the heavens opened. I fetched an umbrella, popped on some Wellington boots and ventured out into the rain. Wet tyres amplified the noise of traffic on the road; people ran into doorways, shrieking and laughing; and I stood, a small puddle forming beneath me, rain hammering down on my umbrella, watching a bee.

I stayed for a while, barely sheltered from the rain myself, while the bumblebee snuggled up in the thatch. She had obviously been there before; parts of the fence had started to become wet but not the area sheltering her. I went inside, occasionally returning to find her still there. The bad weather lasted for hours, and the bee stayed on after the rain stopped, but she will have eventually risen, sleepily hauling herself out of her den and going on her way. I'd never thought of the willow fence as being anything more than a barrier between me and the cycle path beyond the garden, but now I viewed it in an entirely new light: as shelter.

Shelter includes space to hide, breed, feed and hibernate, and can be provided by anything from a pile of plant pots to an old growing bag. Almost every part of your garden may shelter some creature or other; even a well-mown lawn is home to leatherjackets, worms and ants, and so provides dinner for starlings, blackbirds and green woodpeckers. A paved area can be home to ants and centipedes. And a willow fence can shelter bumblebees from the rain.

Yet almost every area of our gardens can be improved for wildlife. A bare fence or wall will provide opportunities for insects to bask in the sunshine, spiders and insects might hide in the cracks, mason bees might make little nests for their young. But if we grow a choice selection of climbing plants up the wall it will come to life: birds may nest in thickets of honeysuckle and ivy, bees and butterflies may feed from the flowers, and moths may lay eggs on the foliage. We can further increase nesting opportunities by adding a bird box and solitary bee hotel (see pages 26 and 28).

Hedges

A mixed, native hedge may attract anything from nesting hedgehogs to birds, bees and butterflies, not to mention all the moths, bugs and flies that so many species rely on for food. Hedges are particularly useful to birds, which may use them to raise young. Birds may also forage from hedges for food such as caterpillars and aphids in summer, and seeds and berries in winter. In addition to that, hedges provide birds with cover to dive into to escape danger; you may find that a bird table placed near a hedge attracts many more birds than one placed in the middle of a lawn with no nearby cover.

Plant a hedge

For the best wildlife potential, choose native plants such as hawthorn (*Crataegus monogyna*), beech (*Fagus sylvatica*), spindle (*Euonymus europaeus*), blackthorn (*Prunus spinosa*), hazel (*Corylus avellana*), holly (*Ilex aquifolium*), field maple (*Acer campestre*) and buckthorn (*Rhamnus cathartica*). You can add interest by growing clematis and honeysuckle (*Lonicera periclymenum*) through the thicket, or planting low growing flowers along the base. Leaf litter allowed to accumulate beneath the hedge will provide shelter for many creatures.

ABOVE *It's not quite a bird's eye view, but this photo of a bird table taken from within a hedge, indicates how a bird might see this potential food source from relative safety.*

TIP

If you can, trim the hedge every other year, as species such as hawthorn and guelder rose flower and fruit on the previous year's growth. Prune in late winter so wildlife can make the most of berries and nuts. Never prune the hedge when birds are nesting.

Climbing plants

The more climbing plants you can grow up your walls and fences, the more shelter you provide. Climbers may also provide nectar and pollen for pollinators, foliage for caterpillars and berries for birds. Here are some you might consider growing in your garden:

CLEMATIS

Some of the best clematis for wildlife include *Clematis cirrhosa* var. *purpurascens* 'Freckles', which produces nectar-rich flowers in late winter, and old man's beard (*C. vitalba*), which offers scrubby shelter, moth food and lovely fluffy seedheads which are not only eaten by goldfinches and greenfinches, but also provide nesting material for a variety of birds. *C. tangutica* and *C. alpina* also have fluffy seedheads. Height up to 30m.

HONEYSUCKLE

Lonicera periclymenum is a beautiful, scented climber with flowers that provide food for long-tongued bumblebees and large moths. Caterpillars of some moths also eat the foliage, while birds eat the sticky red berries. It can be prone to mildew but grows best given a deep root run in partial shade. Height up to 7m.

IVY

Mature ivy (*Hedera helix*) flowers when most other plants have stopped blooming, and has plenty of nooks and crannies to shelter nesting birds and insects. Birds eat the calorie- and nutrient-rich berries. The foliage provides food for caterpillars of the holly blue butterfly as well as several species of moth. Height up to 30m.

RIGHT *Highly fragrant honeysuckle flowers provide food for bees, butterflies, moths and hoverflies, while moth caterpillars may feast on the foliage.*

ROSES

Many single-flowered roses, such as the field rose (*Rosa arvensis*) and dog rose (*R. canina*), are fantastic for pollinators. Single-flowered cultivars like 'Kew Gardens' and 'Rambling Rector' are also excellent. Access to nectar and pollen is difficult in double-flowered cultivars, but the foliage of varieties 'Madame Alfred Carrière' and 'Golden Showers' may be used by leafcutter bees to line their nests. Height up to 6m.

WISTERIA

Wisteria floribunda and *W. sinensis* are great choices for covering east-facing walls, producing beautiful, nectar-rich flowers. Most cultivars have purple flowers, but white-flowered varieties are available. Birds such as blackbirds and robins may nest among the branches. Height 9m.

Compost heaps

The process of decomposition takes place naturally wherever plants grow, but by composting waste we can recreate this cycle in our gardens. A compost heap is nothing more than a pile of rotting plant matter, a central hub where bacteria, yeasts and fungi, and detritivores such as worms, millipedes and woodlice all help return nutrients to the soil.

Because of the smaller creatures a compost heap attracts, it becomes a feeding ground for anything from beetles to birds, slow worms, frogs and hedgehogs.

Composting also benefits us gardeners: organic matter improves drainage, aids moisture retention and aerates the soil. Simply dig it into your borders or apply it to the surface as a mulch, where it will be incorporated into the soil by worms. Blackbirds may also poke through the matter looking for grubs.

Make a compost heap

A large, open pile is the most wildlife-friendly composting option, as it's easily accessible. If you'd rather contain your heap, a slatted wooden box is the next best thing because many species can still access the goods within. Theoretically, a closed, plastic bin is the least wildlife-friendly method of composting. But it needn't be a 'closed shop': simply raise the bin on bricks so that amphibians, reptiles and small mammals can enter and exit easily. These bins can be the warmest of all, so if access is easy, you may attract a family of slow worms.

Position your heap in a sunny part of the garden and add grass clippings and other garden waste (but not the roots of perennial weeds or diseased material), plus cardboard, newspaper and kitchen scraps (including eggshells, vegetable matter, coffee grounds and tea bags but excluding dairy products, cooked food and meat). Keep the waste moist but not waterlogged, and turn the heap to aerate it if it appears to have stopped breaking down. If you do need to turn the heap, try to do so in early spring, as you're less likely to disturb hibernating animals such as hedgehogs, and most species won't yet have started breeding. Always make sure you check the heap beforehand and go in carefully: a garden fork can easily spear an unsuspecting animal sheltering in the waste.

LEFT *These compost bins provide easy access to small mammals and amphibians. Birds, too, may pick through the waste looking for insects. Create as many as you need; while one heap breaks down you can add to another.*

Spent plants

In the wild, plants slowly break down in autumn and winter, helped along by frost and snow. Many have disappeared into the soil or the mouths of earthworms, woodlice and millipedes by spring, and new growth conceals any last skeletal remains. Yet while plants are breaking down, they provide shelter for wildlife such as ladybirds and other insects, which sneak into seedheads and tuck themselves into hollow plant stems or among fallen leaves.

However, in gardens, so many insects end up on the compost heap in autumn and winter, where they might be exposed to damp conditions and therefore put at risk of developing fungal diseases. By simply leaving your borders intact, you can dramatically improve the chances of many species making it through to spring – not to mention earn yourself a grand view of birds eating from the seedheads

you've left standing. You don't need to leave the whole border as it is – maybe you could just clear space around the edges to plant spring bulbs, or leave one untouched area concealed at the back.

ABOVE *The long grass and frosted plant matter at this allotment provide the perfect winter duvet for hibernating wildlife.*
RIGHT *Seedheads of teasel provide shelter for insects as well as nutritious seeds for birds such as goldfinches.*

Leaf piles

A leaf pile replicates conditions found naturally in woodland, where leaves fall from trees and eventually break down to condition the soil. While they're breaking down, they provide habitats and feeding opportunities for wildlife.

The easiest way to make a leaf pile is to gather fallen leaves from your lawn and sweep them under your hedge or to the back of your borders. If you want to harness the soil-conditioning properties of the leaves for use in your garden, you can make a wire cage using wooden posts and chicken wire to make leaf mould. Worms, beetles and other invertebrates should still be able to access the pile easily, as will hedgehogs and amphibians, provided you leave a gap at the bottom (simply cut a 12–15cm-wide hole).

If you don't have a hedge or room for a large metal cage, why not gather leaves from your lawn and pop them into permeable jute sacks (or plastic bags with holes punched in), then store them behind your shed for two years? Applied as a mulch on your borders, the resulting leaf mould will attract a variety of invertebrates, along with the odd blackbird, which may pick through the mulch for grubs. This will give your soil a lovely boost, too.

TIP

Hedgehogs and toads can't tell the difference between a lovely bespoke hibernaculum and an unlit bonfire. Making the bonfire immediately before lighting or even dismantling it and reassembling prior to striking the match can literally save lives.

MAKE A MINI-HIBERNACULUM

'Hibernaculum' is simply the term used to describe the winter quarters of an animal, or where an animal hibernates. It can be anything from a dry-stone wall to a huge leaf pile, but you can create one on a smaller scale using a plant pot and a few fallen leaves. While it's not suitable for larger animals, it may provide short-term shelter for invertebrates (minibeasts), such as beetles.

Simply fill a plant pot with leaves and half bury it in the ground, positioning it to make sure it doesn't become waterlogged. You can provide even more protection by covering the pot with a pile of sticks.

1

2

You will need
**Wooden box (roughly 60 x 40 x 30cm),
or plain, untreated wood (4m of
50 x 25mm and 8m of 100 x 18mm)**
Hinge to fix the lid to the box
Piece of piping for ventilation pipe
**Wire mesh netting to wrap around one
end of the ventilation pipe**
Corner brackets
Newspaper and a few dry leaves
**Drill and wooden drill bits, hole drill
bit, screws**
Jigsaw
Plastic sheeting

*Providing artificial shelter for hedgehogs isn't essential if you already have
a log pile, open compost heap or hedge for them to nest and hibernate in, but
it won't do any harm. You're not guaranteed to attract a tenant, however!*

*There's a wide variety of boxes available to buy, but you can also make
one. Most designs consist of a wooden box with an additional entrance
tunnel. You can use an old wine box or similar if you have one to hand,
or you can make your own using plain, untreated wood (wood preservative
can be harmful to hedgehogs).*

1 Use the jigsaw to make an entrance hole 12 x 12cm at the front of the
box. Use the drill and hole drill bit to make a hole at the back for the
ventilation pipe. Fix the lid to the box using the hinge.

2 Wrap wire mesh netting or similar (I used an old mesh bag) around one
end of the ventilation pipe and fix it using tape. Push the pipe through
the hole so the covered end is inside the box. Angle the pipe downwards
so it doesn't fill with rainwater.

3 Make the entrance tunnel approximately 40cm long, ensuring that the
entrance at each end is 12 x 12cm. Use corner brackets to fix the tunnel
to the box. Line the box with newspaper and add a few leaves to make it
snug. Close the lid.

After you've made your box, cover it with waterproof sheeting such as
pond liner or a sturdy plastic bag, but don't cover the ventilation pipe.
Hedgehog nests are usually found at the bases of hedges or under
bramble thickets, log piles or compost heaps, so ideally place your box
in one of these habitats. Alternatively, pop it in a sheltered corner of
the garden where you can cover it with soil and a thick pile of leaves.

3

Dead wood

Dead wood attracts a lot of wildlife. Simply by leaving tree stumps to rot, and not pruning out all dead material from trees and shrubs, you can provide habitats for a range of invertebrates, including hoverflies and beetles.

Log piles

A log pile positioned in partial to full shade will remain damp and cool, appealing to amphibians and invertebrates such as beetles. Those in sunny locations will warm up and dry out quickly, providing fewer opportunities for amphibians and beetles, but they may attract basking insects and even common lizards. Any wood with bark still intact will offer nooks and crannies to squeeze into.

Stick piles and stumperies

If you don't have room for a log pile, why not gather a few twigs and branches and make a stick pile? Even just a small heap of dead wood can attract invertebrates and therefore provide a feeding ground for birds, frogs and small mammals.

You could also try your hand at making a stumpery. This involves partially burying tree trunks in the ground and planting around them with shade-loving ferns and woodland flowers.

MAKE A LOG PILE

If you have the resources it's a good idea to use wood from local, native trees, but this can be difficult to get hold of, especially if you have a small, urban garden. My log pile is made from Christmas trees, which I rescue from bins and street corners every January. I remove the branches and bind the twiggy brash together with twine, to make smaller invertebrate habitats, and chop the trunk into mini logs. If the best thing you can do is buy a bag of logs destined for a woodburning stove then so be it – this will still make a wonderful habitat.

Pile the logs together in a corner of the garden where they will be left alone. Partially bury the bottom layer if you can, and fill a few gaps with fallen leaves, moss and soil to attract the greatest number of species. You might want to plant clematis or honeysuckle next to the pile, to grow over the logs.

MAKE A MINI-CAIRN

Creating shelter can often help you as much as wildlife. A pile of stones, or mini-cairn, in your border will provide a habitat for frogs, toads and newts, but it will also bring them closer to the slugs and snails eating your plants. The pile may encourage birds – look out for the song thrush, which may use one of the stones as an anvil to smash open snail shells.

To make a mini-cairn, simply choose a variety of rocks and stones and pile them up in your border. You may want to dig a very shallow pit and place some of the larger stones over it this will create cool, damp pockets beneath the cairn, which may be used by toads.

Find a spot in full or partial shade so the cairn doesn't bake whatever is sheltering within it, and leave gaps for wildlife to squeeze through. Mosses and liverworts (see page 50) should naturally colonise the stones, but you could speed things along by adding a little soil and moss if you have some to hand.

Long grass

Left unmown, a grassy strip will quickly erupt into a busy habitat for hundreds of species. Pollinators will visit flowers that may now flourish, while seeding grasses and dandelions will provide food for sparrows and goldfinches. Butterflies and moths may breed in the long grass and hedgehogs, frogs, toads and newts may use it to find food and shelter from predators.

You need only a small strip to make a difference and it needn't be unattractive. Why not make a feature of the habitat, leaving a circle of meadow around a gnarled old apple tree, or cut shapes or create a maze for children?

How often you cut the grass is up to you, but do check the area thoroughly beforehand for sheltering creatures such as hedgehogs and amphibians. You may consider raising the blade height of your mower so caterpillars and other insects can burrow into the thatch.

Plant a mini hay meadow

If you have the space, why not consider converting a patch of lawn into a perennial meadow? Here, a variety of grasses grow alongside wildflowers such as red clover (*Trifolium pratense*), black horehound (*Ballota nigra*), salad burnet (*Sanguisorba minor*), wild carrot (*Daucus carota*) and orchids. A huge number of pollinators will visit the flowers, and the grasses will provide breeding opportunities for moths, butterflies, bees and small mammals. Birds and other predators may also benefit from the availability of prey. There are very few

meadows as a result of increasing pressures put on farmers to maximise productivity. So, by creating one in your garden, you'll do a lot to help wildlife.

Meadows thrive in nutrient-poor soil, otherwise grasses outcompete wildflowers, so if you're starting one from scratch you'll need to get digging. The best way to create a meadow is to completely remove a layer of turf or topsoil up to 10cm. Once you've done this, leave the area for a couple of weeks and remove any weeds that appear. (The longer you leave it, the more weeds you can remove before sowing.) While you're waiting, choose a seed mix appropriate to your soil type and aspect. It's a good idea to include semi-parasitic yellow rattle (*Rhinanthus minor*) in your seed mix, as it weakens grass growth and therefore helps wildflowers to flourish. Prepare the soil by digging it over thoroughly, removing traces of weed roots and raking it level. Broadcast the seed in early autumn.

In the first year, you'll need to cut your meadow three times, to aid root development. Start in spring and mow or strim to about 10cm. Remove all clippings to prevent nutrients from returning to the soil and take out any weeds such as dock, nettles and thistles. Cut again in summer and again in autumn. From the second year onwards, you should need to mow only once in spring and once in autumn, to around 5cm. After the autumn cut, leave the clippings for a few days to allow any remaining seeds to fall.

The wonderful thing about growing a meadow is that it may change each year, as different plants dominate. One year you may have a mini-field of ox-eye daisies (*Leucanthemum vulgare*), another year wild carrot (*D. carota*) may flourish.

ABOVE LEFT AND RIGHT *Self heal and field scabious provide a rich source of food for bees and butterflies.* **OPPOSITE** *A colourful meadow (no matter how large or small) will recreate a valuable habitat that's becoming increasingly rare.*

Bird boxes

More than 60 bird species are known to use nest boxes, with blue tits being the most likely, followed by great tits and coal tits, nuthatches, house sparrows, starlings, robins and house martins. Not only do boxes provide shelter in the breeding season, but birds may also use them to take refuge from the cold in winter. Swifts, house martins, house sparrows and starlings are all in decline, so provision of boxes for them could make a huge difference to local populations.

It's important to choose the right spot for your box, as prospecting birds are unlikely to nest somewhere with strong sunlight, a prevailing wind, or where there's a lot of other bird activity (for example, if the box is too near a feeding station). It's generally advised to place the box in a north-easterly direction, but if tall buildings provide shade and shelter from the wind you needn't stick to the north-easterly rule. If they don't take residence after a couple of years, move the box somewhere else – who knows, for whatever reason the birds might like it better there, even if it's the busiest, noisiest and windiest part of the garden.

Where to site your bird box

Tits	2–4m above ground, such as on a wall, fence or tree.
Robins and wrens	Less than 2m above ground, well hidden but with a clear view.
House sparrows and starlings	Under the eaves of your house – add two or three boxes.
House martins	Under the eaves of your house (away from starlings and sparrows).
Great-spotted woodpeckers	1–3m high on a secluded tree, with a clear flight path.

MAKE A BIRD BOX

Bird boxes are easy to make. Each species has different nesting requirements and no one size fits all, so decide which species you'd most like to cater for before you start. The best time to put up nest boxes is autumn, as it gives birds a few months to become accustomed to the box before the nesting season. Fix the box securely and, if you can, tilt it forward slightly, so any driving rain will not end up in the nest.

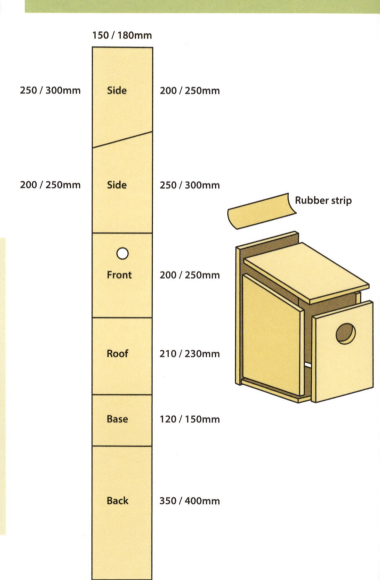

150 / 180mm

250 / 300mm — Side — 200 / 250mm

200 / 250mm — Side — 250 / 300mm

Front — 200 / 250mm

Roof — 210 / 230mm

Base — 120 / 150mm

Back — 350 / 400mm

Rubber strip

You will need

Drill and wooden drill bits

Galvanised nails or screws

Hammer or screwdriver

Rust-proof hinge and catch (optional)

Tacks

**Waterproof material, such as rubber
 (I used a piece of pond liner)**

Saw

Untreated wood at least 15cm x 150cm

The size of the entrance hole should depend on the species you want to attract:

Blue tits, coal tits and marsh tits	25mm
*Great tits, tree sparrows
and pied flycatchers*	28mm
House sparrows and nuthatches	32mm
Starlings	45mm
Great-spotted woodpeckers	50mm
Robins	Open-fronted box
Wrens	Open-fronted box

The plan shows measurements for two sizes of box. Use the larger size for starlings and great-spotted woodpeckers and the smaller size for all other species. Use untreated wood, at least 150mm thick. Treat the outside with a water-based preservative if you like, but don't allow any to leach into the box. I prefer to leave my boxes untreated, as they blend into the surroundings better and also provide a source of wood for social wasps to make their nests. Make your box snug by ensuring there are no draughts, but do drill a few drainage holes in the base. Woodpeckers like to excavate their own nesting cavities, so a woodpecker box should be filled with a block of balsa wood, rotting log or wood chips.

1 Cut your wood to size following either the large or small dimensions on the plan. For an open-fronted box, cut the front panel to 100mm for robins;140mm for wrens.

2 If required, drill an entrance hole in the front panel at least 125mm from the base. Nail or screw the pieces together. If you're making a tit box, don't nail the lid but fix it in place with a hinge and catch instead, so you can get inside to clean it easily.

3 Use tacks to attach a waterproof strip over the hinge or join where the roof meets the back panel, to prevent water entering the nest. Add a few drainage holes to the base and then firmly fix the box to its support, preferably at a slight downwards angle.

Solitary bee habitats

While many species of solitary bee nest in patches of bare earth, natural nesting sites for some include hollow stems and holes made by wood-boring beetles. These can be in short supply in gardens, but you can easily recreate this habitat, known as a solitary bee hotel. Although 'hotel' suggests temporary residence, the bees will reside here for a year, starting off as eggs, which hatch into grubs and then grow, eventually pupating and becoming adults. After spending winter in the box, the adults hatch out, mate and lay eggs of the next generation – often in the same hotel.

All you need is a box or other container filled with hollow bamboo and other plant stems, and wood with holes drilled in them. (If you don't have wood, try using a brick of dry flower-arranger's foam and adding holes using a pencil.)

If you can, add a sloping roof to the box, otherwise fix it to the wall at a slight downwards angle so the holes don't fill with water, and choose the sunniest location possible. Residents are likely to include mason bees, which nest in spring and seal their nests with mud, and leafcutter bees, which nest in summer and seal their nests with rose and wisteria leaves.

In autumn, it's a good idea to take the box down and pop it in a cool, dry spot such as your garage or shed. This is because, in order to survive, the bees need cool and damp shelter in winter. Heavy autumn rainfall can put them at risk of developing fungal diseases. Just don't forget to put the bee hotel back in spring.

ABOVE *You should be able to identify which bees are using your box by the material which has been used to seal the nests. Leafcutter bees use leaves and mason bees use mud.* **RIGHT** *If you grow roses, you might spot semi-circular holes in the leaves, which have been cut by leafcutter bees to line their nests. If you sit and watch, you may see the bees cutting holes out of the leaves, which they roll up and carry to the hotel.*

MAKE A SOLITARY BEE HOTEL

You will need

Saw

Chopped wood or small logs

Selection of plant stems
 (eg, bamboo and sunflower stems)

Sandpaper

Drill and wooden drill bits

Dry flower-arranger's foam (optional)

An untreated wooden box (I used an
 old wine box)

Pencils

Rust-proof bracket

Here I've used an old wine box and filled it with wooden logs, lengths of bamboo and flower-arranger's foam, but you can use any container and any combination of materials, as long as it protects the bees from rain, the wood is untreated and the holes are no bigger than 10mm in diameter. Different species nest in holes of different sizes, so it's worth drilling holes of a variety of diameters (between 2 and 10mm) to attract the widest variety of species.

1. Using a saw, cut the chopped wood or small logs and plant stems to size, softening sharp edges using sandpaper. Drill holes in the wood.
2. Arrange the wood, stems and foam in the box.
3. Once you're happy with the arrangement, make holes in the foam using a pencil or a selection of different-sized pencils. Don't make the holes too wide; the bees will happily excavate their own holes here.
4. Using the bracket, fix the box to a wall or fence in the sunniest part of the garden. You may wish to grow roses or wisteria near the box, to advertise its availability to leafcutter bees, but make sure plants don't obscure the box.

Bumblebee nesters

If you've ever watched a big, fat bumblebee zigzagging over the ground in spring, you can guarantee it will have been a queen searching for a new nesting site. Many bumblebees nest underground in old mouse holes, so a disturbance in the soil or a vague whiff of mouse will instantly be investigated, before the queen moves on, continuing her search. Eventually, she'll find somewhere she's happy with, where she'll make a little wax pot of nectar and pollen before settling down to lay her first batch of eggs.

I've watched many bumblebees prospect for nesting sites in my garden, but none has ever found it good enough. You might be luckier, and you can increase the chances of them setting up home by creating the perfect conditions. Allowing mice and voles to nest in your garden is a good option; but you can also leave a patch of grass to grow long for carder bumblebees, which nest above ground (typically in long, tussocky grass).

Artificial nesting opportunities are also available. However, many shop-bought habitats don't appear to have been designed with the nesting requirements of bumblebees in mind, so it's well worth creating something yourself – success will be measured by how well you can mimic a rodent burrow.

ABOVE *A nest in or near your garden will bring more bumblebees, like this buff-tailed worker, to your flowers.*

TIP

Bumblebees are unlikely to nest in your garden if there aren't any flowers, so grow spring-flowering plants such as willow (*Salix*), crocus, snake's head fritillary (*Fritillaria meleagris*) and hellebores. If they stubbornly refuse to nest with you, at least they'll drop by for a feed.

MAKE A BUMBLEBEE NESTER

This design comprises an entrance tunnel and container to house the nest and keep it dry. Bumblebees don't gather their own material, so you'll need to add this yourself — used pet mouse bedding is a great choice as it gives the nest an authentic smell. While you don't have to make an underground chamber, you do have to convince the queen that the nest is below ground, so a length of hose is essential. Site your nest in a sunny spot at the base of a hedge or fence, and keep your fingers crossed.

You will need

Spade

Stones (optional)

Plant pot, 30cm diameter

Nesting material, such as dry grass clippings and moss or pet mouse bedding

Something to keep the nest together and off the ground (I used an old basket, but you can also make a cradle from chicken wire)

30cm length of hose, 5cm diameter, with drainage holes punched in, to make the entrance tunnel

Piece of slate or broken crock

❶ Dig a shallow pit, adding a few stones for drainage if you have heavy soil. Fill the basket or cradle of chicken wire with dry nesting material and place it in the pit. Make sure the bulk of nesting material is off the ground.

❷ Lay the hose down with one end in the nest and the other where you want the entrance to be. Place the upturned plant pot over the nest, making sure it doesn't kink the hose.

❸ Cover the hose with soil to conceal all but the entrance, and build soil around the hose to deflect rain. Keep this area weed free to make the nest more obvious to prospecting queens.

❹ Protect the nest from rain by placing a piece of slate or crock over the drainage hole of the plant pot. If a queen sets up home and there's space beneath this roof, you may find the workers using it as an additional entrance.

Food

Provision of food often automatically comes with shelter – for instance, a log pile and hedge can provide both. But you can also provide food separately, starting with a few choice plants.

Plants

To you and me, a garden packed with plants is a garden packed with beauty. Plants provide structure, colour, texture, scent and sound. A tree provides something to sit under or even climb. But to wildlife, plants can represent food. What we grow and how we grow it determines how much is available. Choose the widest selection of wildlife-friendly plants possible and you'll be well on your way to having a noisy, bustling garden – a circus of leaf munchers, wood borers, nectar drinkers and everything else that makes up the exciting web of life that's possible outside your back door.

Nectar and pollen plants

There's something almost decadent about lazing in a deckchair on a hot summer's day, half falling asleep to the sound of bees buzzing on lavender. While they're gathering food to take back to the nest, doggedly visiting flower after flower to drink nectar and comb pollen onto little baskets on their hind legs, we're just sunbathing. But this act of lying in the sun listening to bees is one of the most important things we can do, because if we lie in the sun and *don't* hear bees, there's something wrong. At least that's what I tell myself!

Bumblebees, butterflies and moths have suffered dramatic declines in recent years, while honeybees continue to be affected by problems such as colony collapse disorder and the parasitic varroa mite. Many other insects that depend on

ABOVE LEFT *Bees and butterflies can't resist the nectar- and pollen-rich blooms of globe thistles.*

TIP

When choosing nectar plants for butterflies, buy at least three of one type. A large clump of flowers is much more likely to be noticed than one on its own. It's thought that pale coloured plants are more easily found by night-flying moths.

ABOVE *A common carder bumblebee drinks nectar from self heal.*
RIGHT *A small skipper butterfly drinks nectar from bush vetch.*

While nectar is pretty much the same whichever flower it comes from, pollen can vary in quality. Pollen is fed to the grubs back in the nest or hive and – for some species – the quality and amount of pollen they eat can determine their size, health and vigour as adults. Some plants produce top-notch pollen, while others are a bit mediocre. The best source comes from plants in the legume family, including the peas and beans in your veg patch. Red clover (*Trifolium pratense*), kidney vetch (*Anthyllis vulneraria*), bird's-foot trefoil (*Lotus corniculatus*) and tufted vetch (*Vicia cracca*) are also legumes and are therefore excellent sources of pollen.

nectar and pollen – including solitary bees and pollinating beetles – are also declining.

Gardeners can help reverse these declines, simply by growing more flowering plants. It's that easy. The greater the range we grow, the more pollinators we attract.

It's important to provide nectar and pollen for as long as possible. Some bees are now active throughout winter, while other pollinators may emerge from hibernation early, tempted out on warm days in late winter, when food is often in short supply. Then, in autumn, many insects need to build up their reserves before entering hibernation. So just by growing the right plants for as long a season as possible, we can dramatically improve our pollinators' chances of survival (see chart, page 36).

Nectar and pollen offer different types of sustenance, the first is a source of carbohydrate and the second a source of protein. Nectar is essentially sugar and water, and is produced by plants to lure insects to pollinate them. Pollen is roughly equivalent to sperm, and is used to fertilise flowers and produce seed. Bees drink nectar and collect pollen, and in so doing they transfer small amounts of pollen from anthers to stigmas and fertilise the flowers.

Native or non-native?

Many wildlife gardeners extol the virtues of growing native plants, while others claim it's not necessary at all. But, as far as pollinators are concerned, if the flowers have a good source of pollen and nectar which can be accessed easily, non-native plants are great. In fact, non-native plants can extend the season for pollinators, helping those that rise early in the year and go to bed late. Non-European plants that are fantastic for many of our pollinators include anise hyssop (*Agastache foeniculum*), bergamot (*Monarda fistulosa*), Michaelmas daisies (*Aster novae-angliae*), hebes, *Penstemon heterophyllus*, scorpion weed (*Phacelia tanacetifolia*) and *Verbena bonariensis*.

That said, don't lose sight of the fact that our pollinators have evolved a complex relationship with certain plants over millennia, so it's worth growing some native plants, especially those local to you. What's more, some bees are fussier than others, and so feed on a much smaller range of plants than more generalist feeders, which feed on a wide range. These specialists aren't common garden visitors, but if you live near a nature reserve, well-managed arable area or brownfield site, you never know what might turn up. Grow a patch of red clover (*Trifolium pratense*) and keep an eye out for unusual visitors.

Some more exotic plants have evolved to be pollinated by birds. These include kniphofias, phormiums and cannas. Generalist feeders like the honeybee might have a stab at feeding from them, but the honeybee represents a tiny proportion of European pollinators. If you have a small garden, it's best to grow plants that evolved to be pollinated by insects, as they will provide food for a greater number of species.

LEFT TO RIGHT *A honeybee forages from a cranesbill flower. A tree bumblebee gathers pollen from a Welsh poppy. A red-tailed bumblebee flies to viper's bugloss.*

Why pollinators choose certain flowers

Pollinating insects choose flowers that can accommodate their mouthparts or length of tongue (proboscis). You may have a little ginger bumblebee, called the common carder, visiting your garden. This has quite a long tongue, so can reach the nectaries of foxgloves (*Digitalis*) and honeysuckle (*Lonicera*), while those with shorter tongues tend to visit cranesbills (*Geranium*), lavender (*Lavandula*) and daisies. The tongue lengths of butterflies vary too, while hoverflies have a sponge-like proboscis, which they dab over flat, daisy-like flowers. A good rule of thumb is to grow the greatest variety of flowers possible for the greatest number of pollinators.

What not to grow

As well as knowing which plants feed pollinators, it's important to recognise those that aren't so good. Many garden favourites, such as begonias, pelargoniums (often called geraniums), petunias and pansies (*Viola*), are bred to be resistant to disease, flower for a long time, have multicoloured stripes or some other 'wow' factor. They survive well in drought, flower from early summer to the first frosts and provide a cheap burst of colour. However, they don't do

what they're supposed to: feed bees and butterflies. Double-flowered plants are also useless in this respect. Like a closed shop, they may be packed with pollen and nectar, but no one can get to the goods.

ABOVE *The long-tongued common carder has no problem tackling the long corollas (flower tubes) of red clover, which it shares here with a marbled white butterfly (left), or lungwort (right).*

Nectar and pollen plants

EARLY SPRING

Apple (*Malus*)

Bluebell (*Hyacinthoides non-scripta*)

Broom (*Cytisus scoparius*)

Bugle (*Ajuga reptans*)

Cherry (*Prunus*)

Crocus (*Crocus tommasinianus*)

Dandelion (*Taraxacum officinale*)

Grape hyacinth (*Muscari armeniacum*)

Hawthorn (*Crataegus monogyna*)

Heather (*Calluna vulgaris*)

Hellebore (*Helleborus*)

Honesty (*Lunaria annua*)

Flowering currant (*Ribes sanguineum*)

Lady's smock (*Cardamine pratensis*)

Lungwort (*Pulmonaria*)

Oregon grape (*Mahonia aquifolium*)

Pear (*Pyrus*)

Plum (*Prunus*)

Primrose (*Primula vulgaris*)

Red dead-nettle (*Lamium purpureum*)

Rosemary (*Rosmarinus officinalis*)

Snake's head fritillary (*Fritillaria meleagris*)

Sweet William (*Dianthus barbatus*)

Wallflower (*Erysimum*)

White dead-nettle (*Lamium album*)

Willow (*Salix*)

Winter honeysuckle (*Lonicera fragrantissima*)

EARLY SUMMER

Allium

Bellflower (*Campanula*)

Bird's-foot trefoil (*Lotus corniculatus*)

Bush vetch (*Vicia sepium*)

Ceanothus

Chives (*Allium schoenoprasum*)

Comfrey (*Symphytum officinale*)

Cotoneaster

Echinacea

Escallonia

Everlasting pea (*Lathyrus latifolius*)

Foxglove (*Digitalis purpurea*)

Granny's bonnet (*Aquilegia vulgaris*)

Honeysuckle (*Lonicera*)

Kidney vetch (*Anthyllis vulneraria*)

Laburnum

Lupin (*Lupinus*)

Monkshood (*Aconitum*)

Poppies (*Papaver, Meconopsis*)

Pyracantha

Raspberry (*Rubus*)

Red campion (*Silene dioica*)

Rose (single-flowered) (*Rosa*)

Sage (*Salvia*)

Thyme (*Thymus vulgaris*)

Tufted vetch (*Vicia cracca*)

Meadow cranesbill (*Geranium*)

Weigela

White clover (*Trifolium repens*)

Woundwort (*Stachys*)

LATE SUMMER TO AUTUMN

Black horehound (*Ballota nigra*)

Borage (*Borago officinalis*)

Bramble (*Rubus fruticosa*)

Buddleia (*Buddleja*)

Candytuft (*Iberis sempervirens*)

Cardoon (*Cynara cardunculus*)

Catmint (*Nepeta*)

Chrysanthemum

Cornflower (*Centaurea cyanus*)

Cosmos

Dahlia (single-flowered)

Delphinium

Gaillardia

Globe thistle (*Echinops*)

Hebe

Hemp agrimony (*Eupatorium cannabinum*)

Hollyhock (*Alcea*)

Hyssop (*Hyssopus*)

Ice plant (*Sedum spectabile*)

Japanese anemone (*Anemone* x *hybrida*)

Knapweed (*Centaurea*)

Lavender (*Lavandula*)

Lesser burdock (*Arctium minus*)

Michaelmas daisy (*Aster*)

Mint (*Mentha*)

Myrtle (*Myrtus communis*)

Oregano (*Origanum*)

Penstemon

Potentilla

Purple loosestrife (*Lythrum salicaria*)

Red bartsia (*Odontites vernus*)

Red clover (*Trifolium pratense*)

Rock rose (*Cistus*)

Sainfoin (*Onobrychis*)

Scabious (*Scabiosa*)

Scorpion weed (*Phacelia tanacetifolia*)

Sea holly (*Eryngium*)

Snapdragon (*Antirrhinum*)

St John's wort (*Hypericum perforatum*)

Sunflower (*Helianthus*)

Teasel (*Dipsacus fullonum*)

Thistle (*Cirsium*)

Verbena bonariensis

Viper's bugloss (*Echium vulgare*)

CLOCKWISE FROM TOP LEFT *Bluebell. Hoverfly on chrysanthemum. Field scabious. Common knapweed. Peacock butterfly on Buddleia. Echinacea. Bumblebee on lavender. Red campion. Bird's-foot trefoil.*

PLANT UP POTS
FOR POLLINATORS

Container displays are ideal if you're short on space or want to add an extra splash of colour without trampling over your borders. They can also be great for wildlife — choose the right plants and you could have colourful mini pollinator magnets dotted all over your garden.

You will need

Crocks

Pots

Peat-free, multipurpose compost

Plants

These three planting combinations are designed to provide a burst of summer colour. They're not long-term schemes, but you can transfer the plants to your border in spring and use the pots to make a fresh display.

I used three planting combinations:

A *Geranium* 'Dreamland'
Salvia nemorosa 'Schwellenburg'
Sidalcea 'Party Girl'

B *Buddleia* 'Buzz Ivory'
Lavatera x *clementii* 'Rosea'
Verbena rigida

C *Achillea millefolium* 'Red Velvet'
Astilbe 'Bressingham Beauty'
Salvia microphylla 'Hot Lips'

1. Place broken crocks over the drainage holes of your container to stop them clogging up.
2. Half fill the pot with compost.
3. Position the largest plant at the back of the pot, fitting the others in around it. Once you're happy with the arrangement of plants, top up the pot with compost, filling in any gaps and leaving 5cm space beneath the rim.
4. Firm the plants well and water them thoroughly. Allow the water to drain from the pot and then move it to its final location.

MAKE A GREEN ROOF

If your garden is already so packed with pollinator plants that you don't have space for more, why not look to the sky? Green roofs give small gardens a little extra planting space and pollinator food that otherwise wouldn't be there. They also absorb rainfall, which can prevent water from surging into sewers during heavy rain and reduce the likelihood of flooding. Green roofs look pretty, too. In early spring, the roof of my small shed brings primroses to head height, giving me a much-needed boost when so much else is still drab and grey.

You will need

Treated timber batons (I used 2 x 2s)
Tape measure
Protractor
Saw
Sandpaper
Wooden planks (the width will depend on your desired planting depth)
Corner brace brackets and L-shaped brackets
Drill, wooden drill bits and screws
Pond liner
Weed-suppressant material
Green-roof substrate (you can make your own using polystyrene chips, compost and vermiculite)
Lightweight, peat-free compost
Plants
Gravel

This design is for a double-pitched roof on a south-facing shed. It comprises an exterior frame fixed to strong internal supports, so it fits over the roof like a hat. It's planted with sun-loving sedums, which will eventually carpet the whole roof and spill out over the edges. Consider growing a mini-meadow if you have a large roof, or choose shade-loving plants for a north-facing aspect. And it's not just sheds that can be given a wildlife makeover: bird tables, wood stores and even bin stores can also be dressed with a little 'hat' for pollinators.

❶ First reinforce your walls against all that extra wood and soil. Simply screw timber batons into the four corners of your shed.

❷ Measure the length and width of the roof and use a protractor to calculate the angles. Use a saw to cut the wooden planks to size. For a double-pitched shed like this one, you should end up with six pieces of wood. Sand off any rough edges.

❸ Fix the front and back pieces together, using corner brace brackets. Then use L-shaped brackets to fix them to the side pieces. This is your external frame.

④ Screw timber batons to the inside of the frame. These will anchor the frame so it sits on top of the roof, while also concealing it. Calculate how many centimetres are required to conceal the roof and screw your batons above this measurement. If your roof is steep, add a wooden baton across the frame about halfway up on each side, so the compost and plants don't slide down.

⑤ Cut the pond liner to size and place it over the shed, smoothing out any creases. There's no need to glue the liner to a double-pitched roof, as the frame will keep it in place. Liners on single-pitched roofs may slip, so will need to be glued down.

⑥ Carefully lift the frame and place it over the roof, making sure it fits comfortably. Double-check that it conceals

the roof and that there is adequate planting depth for your chosen plants (drought-tolerant sedums need less than 10cm but others require a deeper root run).

⑦ Cut a piece of weed-suppressant membrane slightly larger than the roof and loosely place it in the frame. Add green-roof substrate on top of the membrane, making sure there's a good layer at the bottom where soil and water will be at its highest concentration (for drainage). Fold the edges of the membrane into the frame.

⑧ Place another, smaller layer of membrane over the substrate and tuck it into the frame. Add a deep layer of compost and start adding your plants. Finish with a thin layer of gravel. Water well – the water should run straight out of the bottom of the frame.

Food-plants for caterpillars

Research suggests that some birds in urban areas raise fewer young than those in rural areas, because there are not as many caterpillars and aphids to feed them. As well as tolerating aphids, we can help reverse this trend by growing more caterpillar food-plants. This will boost the amount of food available to hedgehogs, bats and other predators, as well as hungry baby birds. It may also increase numbers of butterflies and moths.

The most common garden butterflies tend to have quite specific breeding requirements – some lay eggs only on large clumps of stinging nettles growing in full sun. Other species, such as the meadow brown and speckled wood, are easier to accommodate as they breed in long grass, so it might be worth trying to attract them instead. If the brimstone butterfly is breeding in your area, you may be able to lure it into your garden by planting buckthorn (*Rhamnus cathartica*) or alder buckthorn (*Frangula alnus*). Luckily, moths tend to be less fussy than butterflies, breeding on a range of herbaceous plants. They are therefore much more likely to breed in gardens.

While many caterpillars are eaten by predators, others will live to pupate into beautiful adults, feed on nectar-rich plants and breed to make the next generation. All in your garden.

BELOW *A caterpillar tucks into foxglove flowers in my garden.*
OPPOSITE *A gatekeeper rests in grass, which it may also use to breed in.*

Encouraging moths

There are so many moths, it's impossible to name them all here, but you should get a good variety if you grow a range of the food-plants listed below. Invest in a moth trap and field guide and see which species you attract.

Apple (*Malus*)
Barberry (*Berberis*)
Bedstraw (*Galium*)
Beech (*Fagus sylvatica*)
Birch (*Betula*)
Blackthorn (*Prunus spinosa*)
Bramble (*Rubus fruticosus*)
Cherry (*Prunus avium*)
Clematis (*Clematis vitalba*)
Currant (*Ribes*)
Dandelion (*Taraxacum officinale*)
Dock (*Rumex obtusifolius*)
Dog rose (*Rosa canina*)
Field rose (*R. arvensis*)
Foxglove (*Digitalis purpurea*)
Fuchsia (*Fuchsia hybrida*)
Hawthorn (*Crataegus monogyna*)
Honeysuckle (*Lonicera periclymenum*)
Hop (*Humulus lupulus*)
Ivy (*Hedera helix*)
Nettle (*Urtica dioica*)
Oak (*Quercus robur*)
Plantain (*Plantago major*)
Plum (*Prunus domestica*)
Primrose (*Primula vulgaris*)
Privet (*Ligustrum vulgare*)
Spindle (*Euonymus europaeus*)
Thyme (*Thymus vulgaris*)
Valerian (*Valeriana officinalis*)
Verbascum (*Verbascum bombyciferum, V. thapsus*)
Willow (*Salix*)

Encouraging butterflies

The following butterflies are all widespread and common and may therefore breed in our gardens if we provide the right habitats for them (although there are generally fewer species in the far north).

BUTTERFLY	CATERPILLAR FOOD-PLANTS
Brimstone (*Gonepteryx rhamni*)	Alder buckthorn (*Frangula alnus*); buckthorn (*Rhamnus cathartica*)
Comma (*Polygonia c-album*)	Nettle (*Urtica dioica*); hop (*Humulus lupulus*)
Common blue (*Polyommatus icarus*)	Bird's-foot trefoil (*Lotus corniculatus*)
Gatekeeper (*Pyronia tithonus*)	Bent (*Agrostis*); fescue (*Festuca*); meadow grass (*Poa*)
Green-veined white (*Pieris napi*)	Garlic mustard (*Alliaria petiolata*); lady's smock (*C. pratensis*); nasturtium (*Tropaeolum majus*)
Holly blue (*Celastrina argiolus*)	Holly (*Ilex aquifolium*); ivy (*Hedera helix*)
Marbled white (*Melanargia galathea*)	Red fescue (*Festuca rubra*); sheep's fescue (*Festuca ovina*); tor grass (*Brachypodium pinnatum*); Yorkshire fog (*Holcus lanatus*)
Meadow brown (*Maniola jurtina*)	Bent (*Agrostis*); cock's-foot (*Dactylis glomerata*); downy oat-grass (*Helictotrichon pubescens*); false brome (*Brachypodium sylvaticum*); fescue (*Festuca*); meadow grass (*Poa*)
Orange-tip (*Anthocharis cardamines*)	Garlic mustard (*Alliaria petiolata*); lady's smock (*C. pratensis*); honesty (*Lunaria annua*)
Painted lady (*Cynthia cardui*)	Thistles (*Cirsium* and *Carduus*); nettle (*U. dioica*)
Peacock (*Inachis io*)	Nettle (*U. dioica*)
Red admiral (*Vanessa atalanta*)	Nettle (*U. dioica*)
Ringlet (*Aphantopus hyperantus*)	Cock's-foot (*D. glomerata*); false brome (*B. sylvaticum*); meadow grass (*Poa*); tufted hair-grass (*Deschampsia cespitosa*)
Skipper, large (*Ochlodes faunus*)	Cock's-foot (*D. glomerata*)
Skipper, small (*Thymelicus sylvestris*)	Yorkshire fog (*H. lanatus*)
Small tortoiseshell (*Aglais urticae*)	Nettle (*U. dioica*)
Speckled wood (*Pararge aegeria*)	Cock's-foot (*D. glomerata*); common couch (*Elytrigia repens*); false brome (*B. sylvaticum*); Yorkshire fog (*H. lanatus*)

Food-plants for birds

As well as growing caterpillar food-plants and tolerating aphids, we can also grow plants to sustain birds through the winter months. Caterpillars, grubs and aphids are hard to find in winter, so birds turn to plants that produce nutritious seeds and fruits for sustenance. They flock to berries of plants such as guelder rose (*Viburnum opulus*), holly (*Ilex aquifolium*) and ivy (*Hedera helix*), fruit of apples (*Malus*) and pears (*Pyrus*), and take seeds from sunflowers (*Helianthus annuus*), teasel (*Dipsacus fullonum*), anise hyssop (*Agastache*) and lavender (*Lavandula*). Berries are particularly important to migrant birds such as thrushes. It's thought that the antioxidants in the fruit help them deal with the physical stresses of their long journey.

TIP

Grow a wide selection of berries to keep birds going through the season. Berries of rowan (*Sorbus aucuparia*) and hawthorn (*Crataegus monogyna*) tend to be taken in early autumn, while holly (*Ilex aquifolium*) and ivy (*Hedera helix*) berries may be left until late winter.

OPPOSITE, CLOCKWISE FROM TOP LEFT *Snowberries. A female blackbird tucks into berries of rowan. A great tit feeds from a sunflower seedhead. Rosehips.*

Encouraging birds

By growing fruiting plants and leaving seedheads standing over winter rather than cutting them back, you'll not only attract more birds to your garden, but you may also save a fortune on bird food.

FRUITING PLANTS

Alder buckthorn (*Frangula alnus*)
Apple (*Malus*)
Blackberry (*Rubus fruticosus*)
Blackthorn (*Prunus spinosa*)
Cherry (*Prunus*)
Cotoneaster
Crab apple (*Malus sylvestris*)
Dog rose (*Rosa canina*)
Elder (*Sambucus nigra*)
Firethorn (*Pyracantha*)
Guelder rose (*Viburnum opulus*)
Hawthorn (*Crataegus monogyna*)

Holly (*Ilex aquifolium*)
Honeysuckle (*Lonicera periclymenum*)
Ivy (*Hedera helix*)
Mistletoe (*Viscum album*)
Oregon grape (*Mahonia aquifolium*)
Pear (*Pyrus*)
Photinia davidiana
Privet (*Ligustrum vulgare*)
Purging buckthorn (*Rhamnus cathartica*)
Rose (*Rosa*)
Rowan (*Sorbus aucuparia*)
Snowberry (*Symphoricarpos*)
Snowy mespilus (*Amelanchier lamarckii*)

Spindle (*Euonymous europaeus*)
Whitebeam (*Sorbus aria*)
Yew (*Taxus baccata*)

SEED- AND NUT-BEARING PLANTS

Alder (*Alnus glutinosa*)
Beech (*Fagus sylvatica*)
Dandelion (*Taraxacum officinale*)
Devil's-bit scabious (*Succisa pratensis*)
Evening primrose (*Oenothera biennis*)
Field scabious (*Knautia arvensis*)

Greater knapweed (*Centaurea scabiosa*)
Hazel (*Corylus avellana*)
Hornbeam (*Carpinus betulus*)
Lavender (*Lavandula*)
Lemon balm (*Melissa officinalis*)
Nettle (*Urtica dioica*)
Oak (*Quercus robur*)
Silver birch (*Betula pendula*)
Sunflower (*Helianthus annuus*)
Teasel (*Dipsacus fullonum*)
Thistle (*Cirsium, Carduus*)
Verbena bonariensis

Weeds

Unfortunately, not all wildlife-friendly plants are beautiful cultivars, resplendent with ornate flowers and jewel-like berries or seeds. Some are a bit ugly. Others are extremely pernicious, spreading like wildfire the minute your back is turned. Yet these plants, or weeds, are often fantastic for wildlife. Rather than exterminating weeds throughout the garden, consider setting an area aside for them, or learn to appreciate their beauty: self heal (*Prunella vulgaris*) and bird's-foot trefoil (*Lotus corniculatus*) can look lovely in a lawn. After all, a weed is just a plant growing in the wrong place. Find the right place, and the wildlife will love you.

The list opposite comprises ten plants that are commonly regarded as weeds. All of them are great for wildlife and, with the exception of bramble, they are fairly easy to remove should you need to. Many thrive in lawns. You can enable these plants to flower by simply mowing less often or raising the height of your mower blade. You can prevent them from spreading to ornamental borders by cutting them down as soon as they've flowered.

Stinging nettles

Because its leaves have stinging hairs, and are therefore avoided by most grazing animals, the common stinging nettle (*Urtica dioica*) is home to more than 40 species of insect – many of which are beautiful garden butterflies and moths. The stinging nettle is also host to the nettle aphid, which emerges earlier in spring than other aphid species, providing an important source of food for ladybirds (which are then already in your garden by the time other aphids arrive). In late summer, birds eat the seeds.

Not every garden is suitable for a nettle patch, but if you do decide to grow one then don't do things by halves. Grow as big a patch as you can afford, in full sun, as many garden butterflies that breed on nettles choose only large clumps in sunny locations (though some species of moth and ladybirds are happier with smaller, shadier clumps). If you can, take seeds or dig up a clump from a patch growing nearby, so you have local nettles for local insects.

ABOVE *Bird's-foot trefoil adds a splash of colour.* **BELOW** *A stinging nettle stands out from the crowd.*

Top ten weeds

❶ Bird's-foot trefoil (*Lotus corniculatus*)
Excellent source of pollen and nectar for bees, and the foliage is a food-plant for caterpillars of the common blue butterfly and six-spot burnet moth.

❷ Bramble (*Rubus fruticosus*)
Moth caterpillars eat the leaves, bees and butterflies visit the flowers, and birds, dormice and butterflies feast on the berries. A dense thicket also provides shelter for hedgehogs and nesting birds.

❸ Chickweed (*Stellaria media*)
The foliage is popular with moth caterpillars, and finches eat its seeds. It's also edible and is delicious in salads. Chickweed self-seeds easily, so just whip out any plants growing in the wrong place.

❹ Dandelion (*Taraxacum officinale*)
This is the larval food-plant of a number of moths, including the white ermine and large yellow underwing. Its flowers are a rich source of nectar and pollen for pollinators, and goldfinches eat the seeds.

❺ Nettle (*Urtica dioica*)
Food for the nettle aphid, nettle weevil, numerous moth larvae and caterpillars of many garden butterflies. Birds, including bullfinches, eat the seeds.

❻ Ragwort (*Senecio jacobaea*)
Provides food for nearly 80 insect species, of which more than 30 depend on it, including the beautiful cinnabar moth. It can be poisonous if eaten by animals, especially horses, so avoid growing it if you live near grazing land.

❼ Rosebay willowherb (*Epilobium angustifolium*)
Caterpillar food-plant of the elephant hawkmoth. Bees and butterflies visit the flowers. It's relatively easy to control; simply remove seedheads before they disperse.

❽ Self heal (*Prunella vulgaris*)
This low growing, spreading weed is common in sunny lawns. Bees and butterflies love its beautiful, nectar- and pollen-rich purple flowers.

❾ Spear thistle (*Cirsium vulgare*)
Caterpillars of many butterflies and moths, including the painted lady, feed on its foliage, and the flowers are a great source of pollen and nectar. Goldfinches eat the seeds.

❿ White clover (*Trifolium repens*)
An excellent source of pollen and nectar for pollinators, particularly bees.

ABOVE FROM LEFT *Kidney vetch and self heal. A small copper takes nectar from a bramble flower. White clover flowers in a lawn.*

Ten trees for wildlife

Trees deserve a special mention, providing food and shelter for a vast number of animals. Not every garden has room for a large tree, such as an English oak (*Quercus robur*), but most plots have space for an apple (*Malus*), or goat willow (*Salix caprea*), which are extremely valuable to wildlife. It's hard to choose just ten trees from the hundreds we could grow in our gardens, as plants that cater for one species might not be so good for another. I've listed ten that support a variety of species. Virtually all of them are good for moths, and the more moths you bring to your garden, the more birds and bats you'll feed, too.

❶ Apple (*Malus*)
Grown on a dwarfing rootstock, many apple varieties are suitable for small gardens. They provide leaves for moth caterpillars, flowers for bees and fruit for birds. The bark is colonised by lichens and is a fantastic host to mistletoe, providing a further source of berries. Cultivated apples seem to be just as good as crab apples. Height 3–6m.

❷ Beech (*Fagus sylvatica*)
Can be grown as a tree in large gardens, or a hedge in smaller plots. Hedge-grown plants retain their autumn leaves, providing shelter for birds. Many moth caterpillars eat the leaves, and birds and small mammals eat the seeds (beech mast) in autumn. Height 10–35m.

❸ Hawthorn (*Crataegus monogyna*)
Grown as part of a hedge, the common hawthorn provides the perfect nesting and roosting opportunities for birds. Bees love the flowers, while moth caterpillars eat the foliage. The berries are an important source of winter food for birds and small mammals. Height 12–15m.

❹ Field maple (*Acer campestre*)
This is perfect for small gardens. Lichens and mosses grow on its bark, moth caterpillars eat its foliage, and bees and wasps visit its spring flowers. The leaves turn a lovely golden colour in autumn. Height 8–14m.

❺ Goat willow (*Salix caprea*)
The catkins provide an early source of food for bees, and moth caterpillars, aphids and other insects eat the foliage. The popular cultivar 'Kilmarnock' is a good choice for tiny gardens, as it grows to just 2m. Average height 6–10m.

❻ Hazel (*Corylus avellana*)
Hazel is a fantastic, dense hedging plant that's ideal for small gardens. The foliage is popular with moth caterpillars, and the catkins provide an early source of food for bees. Squirrels, dormice, great-spotted woodpeckers and nuthatches eat the nuts. Height 12–15m.

❼ Lime (*Tilia cordata* or *T. platyphyllos*)
Lime is suitable for only large gardens. The leaves are eaten by aphids and moth caterpillars, including the spectacular lime hawkmoth, flowers are pollinated by bees, and the seeds are occasionally eaten by birds. The grooved bark provides hibernation opportunities for insects. Height 20–40m.

❽ English oak (*Quercus robur*)
Probably the best tree for wildlife, but you must have a large garden to accommodate it. A mature tree provides shelter and nesting opportunities for birds, acorns as food for birds and small mammals, leaves for moth caterpillars and aphids, and crevices for spiders. Height 15–25m.

❾ Silver birch (*Betula pendula*)
The graceful silver birch is popular with moths, beetles, bugs and sawflies, and therefore blue tits and other insect-eaters. Finches eat the seeds, too. It's slow growing and can be controlled with regular pruning. Height 18–25m.

❿ Yew (*Taxus baccata*)
Several yews can be grown into a beautiful dense hedge, making the perfect nesting and roosting site for birds. The leaves and seeds are toxic, but the flesh of the berries is not, enabling thrushes to disperse the seed without being harmed. Height 4–20m.

Hazelnuts

If you grow hazel (*Corylus avellana*), you can sometimes discover which animals visit your garden by the shells discarded at the base of your hedge. Small mammals, including wood mice, bank voles and squirrels eat hazelnuts, and the way they break into the nut to access the kernel inside indicates which species is feasting in your garden:

- Squirrels tend to split the nuts in half.
- Wood mice cut a circular or ragged hole in the nut and leave tooth marks on its surface and around the edge of the circle.
- Bank voles create a round hole and leave tooth marks across the edge of the circle, but not on the nut's surface.
- Common dormice make a smooth, round hole in the nut, leaving tooth marks visible on the inside.

Woodpeckers and nuthatches also eat hazelnuts – often they take the nuts to a tree where they jam them into a crack and smash them open.

ABOVE *Hazelnuts lie on the ground; some may bear the marks of the animal that broke the nut to reach the kernel.*
ABOVE RIGHT AND BELOW RIGHT *A red admiral butterfly takes nectar from goat willow in spring. Apple blossom provides an early source of nectar and pollen.*

ABOVE *Mosses have colonised this slate roof, growing in large green cushions.* **OPPOSITE TOP** *Lichens and mosses have virtually covered this garden bench. Lichen and navelwort grow on a stone wall.* **OPPOSITE BELOW** *Pleated inkcap mushrooms poke through the grass in a lawn.*

Mosses and liverworts

These are primitive plants, or bryophytes (small plants that don't produce flowers, seed or fruit), and grow in places other plants don't. They're often the first to colonise new spaces, greening roofs and walls that would otherwise remain bare. Along with other 'pioneer species' such as algae, lichens and some weeds, mosses and liverworts take advantage of the lack of competition from taller plants, creating new habitats for invertebrates and ultimately a growing medium for other plant seedlings.

There are hundreds of different species, some of which are suited to growing in lawns, while others form on hard surfaces such as paths, greenhouse glazing, walls and garden ornaments. They spread by microscopic spores blown on the wind and take different forms, with mosses often forming large tufts or compact cushions, and liverworts tending to grow in flatter, fleshier clumps. Some types can be incredibly beautiful: viewed under a magnifying glass, I think ceratodon moss (*Ceratodon purpureus*) looks like a miniature forest. A few clumps are developing nicely on my north-facing garden wall.

Mosses and liverworts thrive in shady, damp conditions and can compete with grass in poorly drained lawns. However, moss is particularly useful to birds, which may scour your garden in spring, taking lumps back to line their nests.

Lichen

Lichens are part algae, part fungi. There are thousands of different types, most of which need clean, unpolluted air to grow. They can grow on bare stone, bird tables, paths, twigs and roof slates, and come in a variety of different colours, from the glorious yellow *Xanthoria parietina* to the sea green *Flavoparmelia caperata*. Caterpillars of some moths, including the marbled beauty (*Cryphia domestica*) and scarce footman (*Eilema complana*) eat lichens, and some birds – including the long-tailed tit – decorate their nests with them.

spores can be distributed by wind, water or even an animal. But these represent a fraction of the whole fungus, which is mostly hidden from view.

Many plants have a mutually beneficial relationship with fungi, which attach to the plants' roots, helping them absorb nutrients. Animals also benefit from the fruiting bodies; wood mice eat some species, and squirrels store mushrooms in trees to eat over winter. A wide variety of fly and beetle species eat and even breed in them.

Fungi

Fungi are neither plant nor animal, and derive nutrients by breaking down plant and animal material, in turn helping turn organic matter into humus, aiding soil structure. Some fungi are parasites, specialising in live plant material, others are saprophytes, living off dead matter.

It's only the fruiting bodies (mushrooms and toadstools) that are visible; they're usually produced on the surface of the food source so their

Feeding birds

So, your garden is packed with natural sources of bird food. In spring and summer, caterpillars feast on your plants, and in winter your herbaceous borders are packed with seedheads and fruiting trees and shrubs. This begs the question: 'If I provide natural food for birds, do I need to supplement it with extra food?' The short answer is yes please, because levels of food in the wild can fluctuate. (For example coal tits and siskins make greater use of gardens when conifer seed crops are poor.) Feeding garden birds is also an absolute joy. Position your feeding station where you can sit and watch from the comfort of your armchair, and keep a pair of binoculars to hand – it's addictive!

Dos and don'ts of bird feeding

DO FEED THEM

- Bird-seed mixes: avoid cheap mixes that contain barley, wheat, split peas or lentils, which tend to be eaten only by larger birds such as wood pigeons.
- Peanuts, preferably chopped and tested for aflatoxin.
- Sunflower seeds: black ones have a higher fat content than striped ones, so are better for birds.
- Sunflower hearts: these require less energy to eat than seeds with husks as the birds don't have to de-husk them in order to eat them, and less waste is generated at feeding stations.
- Niger seeds: popular with goldfinches.
- Fat balls and food bars: add these in winter, as products containing lard and beef suet can melt in summer.
- Live or dried mealworms and dried insects.
- Cooked, unsalted rice.
- Uncooked porridge oats.
- Dry breakfast cereal, preferably unsalted.
- Small amounts of cake and biscuit crumbs.
- Mild, grated cheese.
- Halved apples, soaked sultanas, bananas and other fruit (soak dry fruit to prevent it expanding in birds' guts but avoid leaving out sultanas if you have a dog as they can be harmful to them).

DON'T FEED THEM

- Bread, especially white bread, which fills birds up without providing them with much nutrition.
- Salty food, which can dehydrate them.
- Vegetable, chicken or turkey fat, which can smear on birds' feathers, preventing them from being able to preen or fly.
- Milk, which can cause severe stomach upsets (though a small amount of cheese is fine).
- Desiccated coconut, which can swell in birds' stomachs and cause problems.
- Mouldy food, which can cause respiratory problems.
- Stale food, which can encourage salmonella virus.

Feeding hygiene

Trichomonosis, salmonellosis and avian pox are increasing in some bird species. These are extremely unlikely to be passed to you or your pets, but they can pass between birds whenever they gather to feed, including your bird table and feeders. It's easy to reduce the risk of disease transmission by keeping the feeding area clean. Regularly scrub all items with a suitable disinfectant, rinse well and allow them to dry naturally before refilling. You can use a veterinary disinfectant if you have one (follow the instructions on the bottle). It's also a good idea to move the feeding station around the garden regularly to prevent a build-up of bacteria. If you have a large garden, consider having more than one bird bath and hang feeders in separate places to prevent birds flocking to one small space.

OPPOSITE *A blackbird contemplates a breakfast of seeds.* **ABOVE** *A young blue tit tucks into a meal of fat balls.*

When to feed birds

Traditionally, gardeners were advised to feed birds only in winter, but we're now encouraged to do so year-round. Cater for as many types as you can, for as long as possible.

WINTER
Birds don't hibernate, so forage in all conditions, stocking up on calories for energy to stay warm at night. Because day lengths are so short, smaller birds such as blue tits have a much better chance of surviving if they can fly straight to your garden to eat. Leave food out (such as sunflower hearts and suet-based products) every day, as birds waste energy flying to feeders only to find that they're empty.

SPRING
Parent birds frantically gather aphids, spiders and caterpillars to feed their young, but they also need to feed themselves. Offer a quick snack of sunflower or niger seeds for them to boost their energy levels while foraging for insects. In cold, wet conditions, insects can be hard to find, so a supplementary dish of live mealworms may make a difference to the nesting success of house sparrows.

SUMMER
As baby birds fledge, the number of birds in the garden suddenly explodes (you may spot some birds, such as the great-spotted woodpecker, teaching their young to use feeders). Help fledglings fend for themselves without denying their hungry parents, by leaving out fat balls, niger and sunflower seeds. Many garden birds moult in late summer and lie low to avoid being eaten by predators. Leave food for them at the back of borders, so they can eat in relative safety.

AUTUMN
Birds have to be in peak condition in order to survive winter, so need extra food in autumn to fatten up. Migrants also arrive from colder countries, putting pressure on existing food sources. Migrants are often less used to humans than resident birds, so place food under the shelter of a large shrub or hedge, in which they can hide.

Feeding hedgehogs

A hedgehog's natural diet consists of caterpillars and beetles, plus earthworms, leatherjackets (crane-fly larvae), earwigs, millipedes and slugs. It's a good idea to leave food and water out for hedgehogs in spring, when they emerge from hibernation, and again in autumn, before they go into hibernation, when they will spend four to six months without food. This gives them the best chance of surviving winter and being in a reasonable condition to breed from late spring onwards. You can leave food out for them in summer if you'd like to, especially during dry weather when natural food is scarce. And if you set up a feeding station complete with trail cam, you can get close-up views without disturbing them.

When supplementing a hedgehog's diet, make sure you put food out after sunset, when flies have gone for the night, and remove it as soon as possible the next day. (Fly maggots can be very harmful to hedgehogs.) A dish of drinking water is also essential if you have hedgehogs in the garden. Never give hedgehogs bread and milk as it can dehydrate them and make them ill.

Feeding badgers

Not every gardener is keen on welcoming badgers, as they can dig up lawns looking for leatherjackets, and mess up carefully planted spring bulbs. They can also attack and kill hedgehogs. But if you can live with this then they, too, benefit from additional food and water. Their natural diet consists mainly of earthworms, but they also eat grubs, small mammals and fruit. In dry summers, earthworms retreat deep into the soil, so badgers can go hungry. Place food such as peanuts and raisins in a dish or simply scatter over your lawn. Don't forget a saucer of water.

Feeding foxes

Foxes, like badgers, can cause problems (and may also attack hedgehogs). But they can be fun to observe, so you may want to feed them. Foxes are scavengers, so will eat almost anything, but they're prone to mange, which is thought to be worse in individuals with poor nutrition. Offer them a mixed diet with plenty of protein and vitamins – just leave it in a dish or scatter it over your lawn.

Feeding squirrels

Red squirrels especially benefit from supplementary food, which can help them breed successfully, particularly in areas where greys are abundant. Calcium deficiency can be a problem with reds, which can be exacerbated by sweet or dried foods, so avoid leaving out peanuts, raisins and sultanas. Additional calcium can be gained from a cuttlefish bone or deer antler, if you can provide it. If possible, leave food high up in a tree so the squirrels don't have to cross open ground to access it. Feed them all year round, but only every two to three days, to encourage them to continue foraging in the wild.

OPPOSITE *A hedgehog tucks into a dish of meat-based cat food.*
ABOVE *A red squirrel takes a moment to eat its meal.*

What to feed mammals

MAMMAL	SUPPLEMENTARY FOOD
Hedgehog	Meat-based cat or dog food, especially chicken, rabbit or turkey Meat-flavoured cat or dog biscuits, but avoid fish flavours Specially designed hedgehog biscuits Small pieces of cooked meat leftovers, such as chicken or mince Small pieces of mild cheese Chopped, unsalted peanuts Dry mealworms Sunflower hearts
Badger	Meat-based cat or dog food Seedless grapes or raisins Apples Pears Plums Unsalted peanuts Bread and peanut butter
Fox	Raisins and sultanas (avoid sultanas if you have a dog) Chicken – try chicken drumsticks Fruit, including blackberries and pears Meat-based dog or cat food Raw eggs Bread and butter Bacon Tuna
Squirrel	Beech mast Hazelnuts Pine nuts Sunflower seeds Sweet chestnuts Walnuts Apples Carrots Pine cones

Water

Without doubt, the best source of water in a garden is a pond. Frogs, toads, newts, dragonflies and countless other invertebrates all breed in ponds, but they also provide a host of other species with opportunities for drinking, bathing and even hunting prey.

Ponds are absolutely fascinating, too: sit by one in early summer and you'll see anything from tadpoles 'schooling' like fish to mating dragonflies. You might be lucky enough to see a grass snake swimming across it. Arm yourself with a fishing net and a jam jar and you can discover the magical world beneath the surface – a world of great diving beetles, water hoglice, pond snails and caddisfly larvae. Every garden should have a pond, not just because they're great for wildlife, but because they're enormous fun.

The ideal pond

A typical design for a garden pond is round or kidney shaped with a deep area of 60–90cm for overwintering amphibians, and graduating sides to create shallows. The provision of shallows is probably the most important consideration as so many species – including frog tadpoles – are found only here, living among submerged plants at the water's edge. Hedgehogs and birds also use pond shallows.

If you intend to dig a small pond, a diameter of just 2m with a maximum depth of 30cm will do admirably and will emulate small natural ponds found in the wild. Shallow ponds are more prone to drying out in dry weather however, so you might consider going deeper if you live in an area prone to drought.

For the best results, site your pond in a sunny spot. Not only will this attract a greater range of insects, but it will be more inviting to broody frogs, which prefer spawning in warmer water. Avoid adding fish to your pond, as they can virtually empty it of its tadpoles, nymphs and larvae (although they tend to leave toad tadpoles alone as these are slightly poisonous).

Edging your pond

There's a variety of ways to edge a pond, but if you want to emulate natural conditions then you can't beat a grassy edge. This will grow and provide a refuge for amphibians as they leave the water – especially babies, which are an easy target for birds. Stones and pebbles also make good edging.

More formal edging includes decking or stone slabs. It's a grisly thought, but amphibians can occasionally get stuck to stone as they exit the pond, especially on hot summer days, so opt for decking if you can't be on guard to rescue baking frogs in summer.

If you do choose formal edging, make sure amphibians and other wildlife – including hedgehogs – can exit the pond as easily as they can enter it. Add partially submerged rocks at the shallow end for amphibians and hedgehogs to climb up, or fashion a ladder using plastic coated chicken wire or hessian sacking, which you can then drape over the edge.

OPPOSITE *This pond has a very gradual slope on to a pebble beach so amphibians and hedgehogs can enter and exit easily. The rocks and stones at the edge of the pond offer plenty of nooks and crannies to shelter amphibians.* **ABOVE** *Decking provides a more formal edge to this pond, which frogs like to shelter under in summer. Foliage at the far end also provides cover for amphibians.*

Pond plants

Pond plants provide shelter for tadpoles and other aquatic larvae, as well as a habitat for toads, newts, dragonflies and pond snails to lay eggs. There's an argument for not adding plants to your pond at all, the idea being that the water will quickly be colonised by local plants, with seeds either being carried by the wind or on the feet or feathers of a duck or other pond visitor. This is fine if you live in the vicinity of other ponds (either natural or man-made), but if you're in the middle of a city, or there's no pond for miles, you may prefer to add your own plants. Aim for a good mix of submerged, floating and marginal plants, which provide a variety of habitats for a variety of pond life.

Native or non-native?

I always stick to growing native plants in ponds, as there's no danger of them causing damage to the natural environment if they escape the boundaries of my garden. Native plants have also evolved over millennia with our pond life; I like to think of them as the cosy old armchair that's been in the family for years – they're instantly more familiar and homely than anything exotic and fancy. Many non-native species are incredibly invasive and have the potential to clog rivers and streams, exacerbate flooding and remove oxygen from the water. The worst culprits include floating pennywort (*Hydrocotyle ranunculoides*), parrot's feather or Brazilian water milfoil (*Myriophyllum aquaticum*), New Zealand pigmyweed or Australian swamp stonecrop (*Crassula helmsii*), water primrose (*Ludwigia grandiflora*) and water fern (*Azolla filiculoides*).

Of course, there are lots of non-native plants that don't threaten our natural environment (see list, right), but many pond plants can be pretty vigorous, so if you do grow them, make sure you don't let any escape into the wild and thoroughly compost any material you remove from the pond.

ABOVE *A frog rests in the pond shallows, sheltered by plants.*
OPPOSITE FROM LEFT *Bogbean and water forget-me-not provide shelter for a variety of wildlife, as well as having attractive flowers.*

Five non-invasive, non-native plants

❶ **Blue pickerel/Pickerel weed** (*Pontederia cordata*) – Provides late flowers for pollinators (marginal).

❷ **Dwarf rush/Swordleaf rush** (*Juncus ensifolius*) – Ideal for small ponds (marginal).

❸ **Himalayan marigold** (*Caltha palustris* var. *alba*) – Similar to marsh marigold, but ideal for small ponds (marginal).

❹ **Water hawthorn** (*Aponogeton distachyos*) – Provides surface cover for tadpoles.

❺ **Water lily** (*Nymphaea* 'Hermine') – Provides cover at the surface for tadpoles, ideal for smaller ponds.

Ten native pond plants

❶ **Bogbean** (*Menyanthes trifoliata*) – Dragonflies lay eggs among the leaves (marginal).

❷ **Brooklime** (*Veronica beccabunga*) – Newts lay eggs in the leaves (marginal).

❸ **Flag iris** (*Iris pseudacorus*) – Dragonfly nymphs use the stems to exit the water (marginal; suitable for large ponds only).

❹ **Frogbit** (*Hydrocharis morsus-ranae*) – Floating plant that shelters tadpoles from predators and is a good alternative to water lilies for small ponds.

❺ **Hornwort** (*Ceratophyllum demersum*) – Provides underwater cover for newts, frogs and toads and absorbs excess nitrates in the water, preventing the spread of algae.

❻ **Marsh marigold** (*Caltha palustris*) – Toads lay spawn around submerged stems and dragonfly nymphs use them to climb out of the pond (marginal).

❼ **Starwort** (*Callitriche palustris*) – Offers surface protection for tadpoles and absorbs excess nitrates in the water, preventing the spread of algae.

❽ **Water forget-me-not** (*Myosotis scorpioides*) – Newts lay eggs in the leaves (marginal).

❾ **Water lily** (*Nymphaea alba*) – Newts shelter under them and honeybees use them as landing pads through which they can drink water.

❿ **Water soldier** (*Stratiotes aloides*) – Floating plant that protects tadpoles from predators; a good alternative to water lilies for small ponds.

MAKE A SMALL, SHALLOW POND

This is one of the easiest ways to create a wildlife pond as its shallow depth means you don't have to dig much! Choose an open, sunny site if possible, work out how much space you have and whether you want a formal pond or a more natural-looking one. If you opt for a natural edge then all you have to do is lay turf around the pond, preferably ensuring that some of the turf is in contact with the soil. This might turn yellow at first, but it should survive, and the shallow root run will prevent the grass from growing too long.

You will need

**String and a piece of bamboo,
   or hosepipe and sand, for marking
   out the site**

Spade

**Spirit level and plank of wood
   for checking levels**

Craft knife or scissors

**Butyl liner and underlay (if you don't
   want to buy underlay, use sand or an
   old carpet)**

Turf to hold the liner in place

Pond plants

Gravel

Large stones or log (optional)

This pond has a diameter of just 2m and a maximum depth of 30cm. I dug it into a south-facing border on the edge of the lawn, so on one side I was able to simply pull back a section of lawn and bury the liner beneath it. I laid turf to keep the rest of the liner in place, and replaced the border plants I had previously dug up to create a densely planted habitat to protect emerging frogs.

1 Start by marking out the shape. I made a basic circle using a piece of bamboo and a length of string, but you could use sand or a hosepipe to mark yours. You don't have to make a circle; be as creative as you like.

2 Start digging from the centre, working your way out. Don't dig any deeper than 30cm. If you're going to add plants, create a shelf for them along one side, making sure the shelf is wide enough to accommodate all of your planting baskets.

3 Level the edges of the pond, making sure there are no
steep ridges, and remove any sharp stones you find as
you go around. Lay a plank of wood across the pond
and use a spirit level to check that the sides are level.

4 Cut the underlay and liner to size, cutting more than
you need (use two layers of underlay if you can). Lay the
underlay down, smoothing out any lumps or bumps,
then add the liner. Use a soft broom to get into any
corners and remove creases.

5 Replace turf if you have dug into a lawn, or cut turves
to size and position them around the edge of the pond
to keep the liner in place. You might want to add a few
rocks or large stones, or a log to finish the pond.

6 Add water from your water butt or wait for rain. Once
the pond has partially filled, add your plants. Pot up
marginals in planting baskets topped with gravel and
place them on the shelves. Add floating and submerged
plants to the water.

Container ponds

If you have a really small garden, you don't need to dig a pond at all. Mine is made from an old tin bath. It's not teeming with wildlife, but it's perfect for my rescue frogs and is also home to pond snails, water hoglice and other invertebrates. Birds occasionally bathe in it, too. The bath is lined with mud and plants to recreate the shallows found in natural ponds, and I've added a 'frog ladder' of stones outside the bath, for easy access.

Tap water or rainwater?

It's best to use rainwater to fill a pond, either allowing it to collect gradually or using water from a butt. Tap water may contain chlorine and chloramines, which are harmful to aquatic life. Chlorine breaks down after 24 hours, but chloramines take a lot longer. If you really have to use tap water, find out if your water supplier adds these harmful chemicals to your mains supply and act accordingly.

ABOVE *Container ponds like this tin bath can provide a habitat for a variety of wildlife, including common frogs and some dragonflies.*
RIGHT *Common frog tadpoles are usually found at the shallow edges of ponds, sheltering among submerged plants.*

HELP!

My pond is full of leaves. Will it harm wildlife?

Yes and no. Most ponds have a bit of natural sediment, including fallen leaves, twigs and branches. Indeed, fallen leaves make a good habitat for hibernating frogs and even a nice coat for caddisfly larvae. However, a large amount of leaf-fall in ponds can upset the pH balance of the water and may contribute to the build-up of noxious gases under ice (which may poison frogs hibernating at the bottom).

What can I do? Try to achieve a balance. If you do decide to clear out your pond, do so in autumn, as this causes the least disturbance to wildlife. There's no need to change the water, simply use a net to retrieve leaves from the surface (or the bottom, if you think there are too many), and let the water settle back down. If you need to make repairs to your pond, try to collect as much water as you can and return it to the pond when you've finished. Any aquatic larvae can also be rescued and returned. Make piles of collected leaves around the pond for any creatures to crawl back into the pond, and double-check for stragglers before popping the leaves on the compost.

Why are there still tadpoles in my pond in autumn?

Tadpoles have usually developed into young adults by mid-summer, but it's not uncommon to find tadpoles in the pond in autumn. Reasons could include a lack of food due to a particularly large amount of spawn laid, or cold water due to a lack of light reaching the pond. If the tadpoles survive winter they will complete their development and leave the pond in spring.

What can I do? If the pond is in the shade, consider cutting back any trees or shrubs that block the light, as this will help the water maintain a warmer temperature next year.

ABOVE *Fallen leaves provide the perfect landing pad for mating insects, like these two pond skaters.*

The ice on my pond has thawed and the water is full of dead frogs.

This is extremely distressing, but it's perfectly normal. Frogs (particularly males) may spend winter at the bottom of ponds, breathing through their skin. A thick layer of ice can form over the pond during prolonged cold periods, which prevents noxious gases, formed as plant debris breaks down, from leaving the water. These gases can then poison the frogs, known as 'winterkill'.

What can I do? You can try to prevent it from happening again by removing some leaf litter and other debris from the pond in autumn, and making sure there are plenty of oxygenating plants in the water. After heavy snowfall, remove snow from the ice to ensure light can penetrate the plants (this will encourage them to photosynthesise, producing oxygen). You can also rest a saucepan of boiled water on the surface of the pond to melt a hole in the ice. (It's easier to do this before a thick layer builds up, and you'll need to do this regularly to stop the hole freezing over again.) Never smash the ice, as this can shock and kill any frogs or other creatures in the pond.

Water 63

Bog gardens

Like ponds, bog gardens are good for bats, as they provide a habitat for the aquatic larvae of insects, which bats eat. While gardening for midges and mosquitos might not be high on your list of priorities, these and other insects provide bats with the energy they need to survive. Many bat species, like other insectivores including swifts and sparrows, are declining, due to a lack of insect food. The more insects we can create habitats for in our gardens, the more food we provide for declining species.

Bog gardens are a great option if you have a small garden, as you can create homes for amphibians and food for pollinators, birds and bats in one area. You can either add one alongside your pond or create one in its own right.

Create your bog garden in the same way you would create a pond (see page 60), only much shallower (about 20cm deep). Pierce a few holes in the liner and add a layer of gravel for drainage if you have particularly heavy soil. Place a layer of soil over the top of the gravel to which you add your plants.

ABOVE *Teasel provides nectar- and pollen-rich flowers for a variety of pollinators in summer, and nutritious seeds for birds such as goldfinches in winter.* **BELOW** *Ragged robin is a beautiful plant that's also popular with bees and butterflies.*

Ten bog garden plants

❶ Devil's-bit scabious (*Succisa pratensis*)
❷ Hemp agrimony (*Eupatorium cannabinum*)
❸ Lady's smock (*Cardamine pratensis*)
❹ Marsh mallow (*Althaea officinalis*)
❺ Meadowsweet (*Filpendula ulmaria*)
❻ Pennyroyal (*Mentha pulegium*)
❼ Purple loosestrife (*Lythrum salicaria*)
❽ Ragged robin (*Lychnis flos-cuculi*)
❾ Teasel (*Dipsacus fullonum*)
❿ Water avens (*Geum rivale*)

Bird baths

A bird bath makes a fantastic addition to a garden, even if you already have a pond. Not only do birds drink from them, but they use the water to clean their feathers. Hedgehogs also drink from bird baths if they can access them, while frogs might sit in them (although this isn't particularly sensible, as quite a few birds eat frogs). Honeybees, wasps and other insects also drink from bird baths, so add a few stones around the edge to enable them to exit easily. If you have space, dot a few baths around the garden. Choose pedestal baths as well as those that sit on the ground. Baths that hang from trees are also popular.

BELOW *A dunnock cautiously enters the water to take a drink and clean its feathers.*

Pest control and pesticides

In the Hanyuan County of Sichuan Province, in western China, fruit growers hand-pollinate their pear trees. The process is labour intensive and costly, but the farmers have no choice; if they didn't pollinate the trees by hand, they wouldn't have any pears. Not only have pesticides wiped out natural pollinators in the area, but many local beekeepers have moved their hives out of the county for fear of losing their bees, due to continued pesticide use.

I'm sure we've all stepped into the garden to find a tray of seedlings reduced to little slimy stumps by slugs or snails, or picked up a special plant to find it no longer has any roots because they have been eaten by vine weevil larvae. At these times, it's tempting to reach for the chemicals. But chemicals do so much more than remove one or two specific troublemakers from the garden. At best, they take a few other creatures out as well as the intended recipient; at worst, they knock the whole garden ecosystem out of kilter.

Bug sprays are used to kill a range of insects, including aphids, mealy bugs and lily beetles. But if you zap a cluster of aphids on your broad beans, you're also likely to take out their insect predators – the ladybirds and hoverflies. Most ladybirds and hoverflies breed only once a year, whereas aphids breed constantly throughout summer (in fact, some can reproduce without mating). So if you kill the aphids, hoverflies and ladybirds, you're actually creating the perfect conditions for aphids to breed without any threat from predators at all. Then you take on the role of the predator; regularly spraying the aphids to keep numbers down. You become reliant on the bug spray, spraying more and more to keep the aphids in check. It's a vicious circle that will ultimately lead to only one thing: pollinating your crops by hand.

It's not just bug sprays. Hang a piece of sticky fly paper in your greenhouse and you'll catch and kill anything from whitefly to hoverflies, bees and butterflies, even small birds. Scatter slug pellets around your hostas and you run the risk of harming the song thrushes and hedgehogs that eat slugs

and snails. Add a vine weevil drench to your container-grown plants and you may see fewer bumblebees in your garden next year. On top of that, all of these 'pests' are food for some creature or other.

This all sounds very dramatic. And it might seem silly comparing the effects of widespread pesticide use in China with small-scale spraying in our ornamental borders, vegetable patches and greenhouses. But pesticide use is rife the world over, covering large areas of farmland. This, surely, is reason enough not to use them in our gardens – together, we can create the biggest nature reserve in Europe.

BELOW *A closer look at this sticky trap reveals bumblebees, butterflies and hoverflies, as well as the usual gamut of flies and other insect 'pests'.*
OPPOSITE *A butterfly drinks nectar while a bumblebee gathers pollen.*

Neonicotinoids

Since the 1990s, a group of pesticides has been used that has been linked to bee deaths, particularly colony collapse disorder. Known as neonicotinoids, these pesticides are systemic, meaning they're absorbed into every part of the plant. The chemicals are often applied as a coating to seeds so as the plants germinate and grow, they absorb the chemical, providing protection against insects that eat the leaves or roots. Unfortunately, the chemicals are also taken into the pollen and nectar of the plants' flowers. While the chemicals are present in extremely small doses, one bee can visit a thousand flowers a day, collecting pollen and nectar to feed the grubs. One colony of bumblebees can contain up to 300 workers, while a honeybee hive houses up to forty thousand bees. If each worker visits a thousand neonicotinoid-treated flowers every day, then soon you have a large concentration of pesticide residue back at the hive or nest.

A study conducted in Scotland in 2011 showed that bumblebee nests exposed to neonicotinoids produced 85 per cent fewer queens than those not exposed to the pesticides. The bumblebee lifecycle is annual; daughter queens are produced in summer, before the original queen and workers die. The new queens mate and build up their fat reserves before hibernating and then each one starts a new nest in spring. In summer, each queen produces her own daughters to continue the cycle the following year, before she and the rest of her nest die.

The six months between mating and starting a new nest are already perilous for daughter queens. They may not be able to build up enough fat reserves so they die of starvation, or they may be disturbed during winter, or frozen to death or even flooded if they don't choose a good hibernation spot. A reduction of 85 per cent in the number of daughter queens could mean that no queens from the original nest produce a new colony the following spring. Ultimately, this could lead to extinction.

Another study showed that honeybees exposed to neonicotinoids were less able to navigate back to the hive, resulting in less food for the grubs, lost workers dying and the colony dwindling in size. This could explain, or at least contribute to, the phenomenon known as colony collapse disorder, where beekeepers find their hives deserted.

At the time of writing, use of neonicotinoids is limited in some parts of Europe but further evidence is needed to persuade other governments to follow suit. Manufacturers of the pesticides have denied a link between bee declines and neonicotinoids, having conducted their own tests.

Regardless of what our governments and the manufacturers say, it's clear that use of these pesticides *may* be linked to bee declines. While further research is done, we can all ensure that bees can forage without any exposure to neonicotinoids in our gardens, by not using pesticides.

Alternatives to using pesticides

As we already know, ladybirds and hoverflies eat aphids, and many birds – particularly the house sparrow – feed them to their young. Caterpillars, too, are eaten in their thousands every spring.

I rarely see aphids in my garden, and caterpillars don't get much opportunity to eat my plants when the great tits are breeding. I used to have a problem with vine weevil but don't anymore, thanks to the frogs, which also do a brilliant job of keeping the slug population in check. But I do wish something would eat the snails. Sometimes I feel like my garden is the meeting place for the local Snail Association. In spring, I imagine the snails of London making some sort of annual pilgrimage to my garden; on their way they discuss the havoc they can wreak when they finally arrive. I find it frustrating, time consuming, even heart wrenching, but that's snails; they eat your plants.

My favourite way to deal with snails is to take them 'on holiday'. I gather them up in a bucket and carry them to the wildlife area in the local park. Some will no doubt thrive and

breed, while others will be eaten by song thrushes and other predators, which rarely come into my garden. The snails would have to be pretty determined to return – a train track, road and busy cycle path lie between them and my plants.

The main thing is to relax. If you see aphids on your broad beans, don't panic. Don't squish or spray immediately, but sit back and see what happens. The predators will likely find them in due course. If, after a couple of weeks there are still no predators picking off your aphids, then go ahead, squish a few. But try to make sure you're not also killing the larvae of ladybirds, and that there's still enough to feed the more well-behaved wildlife you do want to attract.

Organic methods of pest control

What you do with pests is up to you. Some gardeners are happy killing them, while others prefer to accept a few plant losses or take pests such as slugs and snails 'on holiday' (as I do). Regular patrols can help limit damage and keep populations in check. Over time, a balance may be achieved by increasing habitats for their predators.

SLUGS AND SNAILS

- Conduct regular night-time inspections and remove slugs and snails by hand.
- Sink cups of beer into the ground; slugs and snails will be attracted to it and will drown (ensure the traps are proud of the soil's surface to stop ground beetles falling in).
- Apply nematodes (naturally occurring slug parasitoids) to the soil in spring and autumn to reduce slug populations without harming other wildlife.
- Create hiding places for slugs and snails near vulnerable plants, which you can check daily. Simply leave out a piece of slate or broken plant pot to create damp, dark shelter.
- Install physical barriers, such as copper rings or plastic cloches, around your plants.
- Use rings of grit, crushed eggshells or spent coffee grounds.

LEFT *Slugs and snails suffer a mild electric shock when they come into contact with copper rings, placed here to protect these young plants.*

TIP

One of the easiest ways to control greenfly and blackfly is to grow a patch of nettles. This will attract the nettle aphid (*Microlophium carnosum*), which emerges earlier than other aphids, giving ladybirds a head-start on potential infestations in your garden.

APHIDS

You can use an organic soap spray, squish them with your fingers or blast them with a jet from your hose, but try to avoid doing so if you have nesting birds in the garden, and do check that ladybirds and hoverflies haven't already moved in.

CATERPILLARS

Remove caterpillars by hand and place them on the bird table. Alternatively, you can transfer the caterpillar to another host plant (elephant hawkmoths, for example, can be moved from fuchsias to rosebay willowherb).

VINE WEEVIL

Regularly checking vulnerable container-grown plants can make a huge difference. Look for signs of eggs or larvae, and transfer these to your bird table, removing adults as and when you find them. Apply nematodes to container-grown plants in spring and autumn to kill the larvae.

LILY BEETLE

In many parts of Europe, there are four parasitic wasps to keep lily beetle numbers under control, but there are far fewer predators outside the beetle's natural range. The easiest way to get around the problem is to stop growing lilies, but if you don't want to do that, you'll need to regularly remove adults and larvae by hand.

ABOVE RIGHT *The crocodile-like ladybird larvae (left) takes a rest while aphids (right) gather on the growing tips on a young rose leaf.*

Keeping a natural balance

If you've always used pesticides and suddenly stop, you're going to experience an explosion of aphids and other pests before the predators return to keep them under control. Unfortunately, this is inevitable and necessary, as it will take time for the natural balance of your garden to be restored. Other factors, such as the location of your garden and the weather, can also play a part in the fate of your plants. For example, if you live in a city you may not have a local population of hedgehogs to eat your slugs and caterpillars, and a wet summer is all that's needed to ensure you're overrun with slugs and snails. But your garden should right itself in time. In the meantime, use organic methods of control, but make sure you don't remove all pests, otherwise there will be no food for the frogs, birds and hedgehogs you want to attract. Sometimes, you'll need to tolerate a little plant damage.

Discovering which wildlife visits our gardens is great fun, but it also helps us appreciate the habitats we've created. We can then add to these habitats to meet the specific needs of other species that might also be lured in.

Identifying species helps us spot behaviours, such as how a blackbird hops about a lawn flicking his tail. It can also help us care better for certain animals; if we find a newt under a stone we know it's likely to be hibernating and therefore doesn't need returning to the pond.

We can use this knowledge to become citizen scientists. There are many surveys to take part in, from garden birdwatches and butterfly counts to whole BioBlitzes where you spend 24 hours counting species in your garden. This information helps scientists monitor populations and offer advice that will help us become better wildlife gardeners.

I can't list them all, but here are some of the more common species to get you started.

2 Mini field guide

Birds

Birds are some of the most obvious garden visitors. If you have a good mix of trees and shrubs, natural food and a feeding station complete with bird bath and a selection of supplementary food, you could attract around 30 different species.

Identifying most garden birds is relatively easy. If you're a complete beginner I think it's a good idea to start in winter, as most birds will by then have their adult plumage, making each species more recognisable. They will also be concentrated around your bird feeders, so you can sit in the warmth of your home with a pair of binoculars and a field guide, learning the different colours and behaviours of each species.

Look out for ground feeders such as robins, blackbirds, wrens and thrushes, and birds that visit hanging feeders, including tits and finches. Berry-bearing shrubs such as hawthorn, guelder rose, holly and cotoneaster may attract blackbirds, robins, song thrushes, bullfinches and starlings. (For a full list of fruiting shrubs to plant for birds see page 44).

RIGHT *Blue tits will be attracted to peanut feeders.* **OPPOSITE** *This baby robin hasn't yet developed its adult feathers.*

Ten things to do for birds

❶ Mulch borders with leaf mould for blackbirds.

❷ Mow your lawn at different lengths – short for blackbirds and starlings, longer for insect-eaters like sparrows and seed-eaters like goldfinches, which love dandelion seeds.

❸ Plant a variety of shrubs and trees, or a hedge, including leafy broad-leaved trees to attract insects and those that produce fruit (see page 44).

❹ Cover walls and fences with a variety of climbing plants.

❺ Make a log pile.

❻ Put up bird boxes, choosing designs that meet the needs of a variety of species and installing them in appropriate locations (see page 26).

❼ Dig a pond and/or install a bird bath.

❽ Grow a variety of caterpillar food-plants (see page 42).

❾ Provide supplementary food all year round (see page 52).

❿ In dry springs, keep an area of bare earth well watered to provide mud for nest-building house martins.

HELP!

There's a baby bird on my lawn. Should I take it in and care for it?

No. The parents are usually very close by and it's very unlikely that they will have abandoned their baby. The young of many species fledge after they've grown feathers but before they can fly, so the baby could just be spending a couple of days on the ground until it's fully developed.

What can I do? If you have a cat, keep it indoors until the bird has flown. If you think the bird is in a particularly vulnerable position, you can move it to a more appropriate place, but don't move it too far away or the parents won't be able to find it (touching a bird won't make its parents abandon it). Otherwise, just keep an eye on it. If the parents don't return, call your local wildlife rescue centre.

Bird migration

More birds migrate than you might think – indeed, our gardens could be compared to airport terminals; no sooner has one lot of birds arrived than another departs. Common species that come to Europe from Africa every spring include the swallow, swift, house martin and cuckoo. They quickly feed to replenish lost energy reserves, raise young (or in the case of cuckoos, let another species do all the hard work), and then return to Africa for winter.

Winter migration usually starts in early autumn. A wide range of birds, including finches and members of the thrush family such as the redwing, fieldfare and blackbird, head west to the UK, Ireland and even Iceland from Russia and northern Scandinavia in winter. These birds may behave a little differently to resident birds, as they're often less used to gardens and being in close proximity to humans. If you do spot such shy-looking birds in your garden, consider leaving water and food for them at the base of a hedge or at the back of a border – they may be too timid to visit your feeders and will be hungry after their long journey.

British residents may stay put, fly to a warmer part of the country or head to the continent. Goldfinches are known as partial migrants; in any given winter, some individuals fly south while others remain here - each individual makes its own decision based on food availability, weather conditions and how much competition it faces from other birds.

Birdsong

To you and me, birdsong is a wonderful consequence of gardening for wildlife, gladdening the heart in spring with the promise of new life. Yet for birds, their song is far from joyful – it's a vital tactic used by males to aggressively mark territories, woo mates and perhaps even ward off threats to their paternity. As such it's a hard job and could be the reason why males of some species don't help with nest building or incubating the young – they're far too busy!

Yet, leave your bedroom window open at night in spring and you may be woken at 4am by the beautiful call of a lone blackbird or robin, perhaps singing to tell the world that he's survived the cold night and therefore his girlfriend is still spoken for. These lone voices are soon joined by those of song thrushes, wrens and wood pigeons, building up to a deafening crescendo that includes late risers such as dunnocks and chaffinches. I think it's one of the loveliest ways to wake up, but I've known gardeners who would rather get a little more sleep than these noisy males allow them.

Blackbirds and song thrushes are known for their beautiful melodies, but small birds can also belt out a good tune. I particularly like the song of wrens, great tits and dunnocks. Starlings are fantastic mimics and have been known to imitate the sound of fire engines, burglar alarms and even other birds. By comparison, I think the bullfinch sounds a bit weak and half-hearted, but it makes up for this in beauty.

HELP!

Where have all the birds gone?

After breeding, many garden birds moult. During this period they're less able to escape from predators, so they lie low until they've grown their winter plumage. There's also an abundance of natural food in the trees, fields and hedgerows in late summer, as grain, berries and fruit ripen. So birds are likely to be less dependent on your garden.

What can I do? Nothing, they will soon be back, although this might be the perfect opportunity to give feeders a good clean.

OPPOSITE *The call of a male blackbird may be the first thing you hear each day in spring. If he doesn't find a mate he may sing throughout summer.*

Great-spotted woodpecker (*Dendrocopos major*)

Predominantly a woodland bird, the great-spotted woodpecker will also visit gardens, especially if there are peanuts going!

It's often heard rather than seen; males drum on trees to attract a mate or advertise a territory. It's about the size of a blackbird, mainly black and white with a red patch on the underparts, just before the tail. The male has a red mark on the back of his head and juveniles have a red crown.

The great-spotted woodpecker eats insects and their larvae, which it probes from tree trunks with its long, sticky tongue. It also feeds on nuts and berries, and sometimes bird eggs and nestlings (it can break into bird boxes by drumming the wood to increase the size of the entrance hole).

Nests are made in holes excavated in trees, and the female lays one brood of five or six eggs. Both the male and female incubate the eggs for 10–13 days, and the young fledge after 20–24 days.

How to attract them If you have the space, grow broad-leaved trees where great-spotted woodpeckers can forage for insects, and keep feeders well stocked with peanuts.

Sparrowhawk (*Accipiter nisus*)

The sparrowhawk is a magnificent creature. While some people may find the sight of these birds of prey upsetting because they hunt and seize smaller birds, their presence is a sign of a healthy bird population.

Mostly grey in colour, adults have a grey hooked beak, a pale, barred underbelly and spindly yellow legs. Females are bigger than males, so prey on larger birds, including thrushes, starlings and pigeons, while males stick to tits and sparrows. Small mammals may also be taken.

Nests are made from twigs and built in trees or large, thorny bushes. The female has just one brood, usually laying up to four or five smooth, bluish eggs. These are incubated for up to 36 days and the young fledge after a further 24–28 days.

How to attract them Encourage a healthy garden bird population. If you'd rather deter them, site a feeding station near a dense hedge, for small birds to escape to quickly.

ABOVE *A sparrowhawk surveys the landscape.* **RIGHT** *A female great-spotted woodpecker clings to a tree trunk.*

Green woodpecker *(Picus viridis)*

The green woodpecker is green with a yellow rump, red crown and whitish underparts. Males and females are similar although the female has a black 'moustache' while the male's is red with a black edge.

Although it drums on wood like other woodpeckers, it's more likely to be seen on the ground, foraging for ants on lawns. The green woodpecker will also eat other insects, and occasionally fruit and seeds. It has a loud, laughing call, which inspired one of its English common names, the 'yaffle'.

Nest holes are excavated in trees, usually by the male. The female lays five to seven eggs and both adults incubate them for 17–18 days. The young fledge after 23–27 days.

How to attract them Keep your lawn well mown and don't discourage ants.

ABOVE *A male green woodpecker, identified by its red moustache with black edge, in the perfect location for finding an ant or two.*

TIP

You can deter great-spotted woodpeckers from breaking into bird boxes by adding a metal nest hole protector to the outside. This simply screws on and prevents woodpeckers from increasing the size of the entrance hole to gain access to the chicks.

Swift *(Apus apus)*

The swift is a wonderful bird. A brilliant flyer, it eats and sleeps on the wing and drinks by catching raindrops in the air. It only comes to earth to nest.

It's brown-black with a faint white patch on the throat, but is best identified by its scythe-shaped wings and screeching calls as it races through the air in little gangs. The swift eats invertebrates, including aphids, and airborne spiders. Nesting pairs mate for life, migrating from Africa to the same communal site each year to raise young, before flying back to Africa.

Nests are made from feathers, paper and leaves in the roof space of houses and other tall buildings, or in bespoke nest boxes. Two or three eggs are usually laid, which are incubated for 19–20 days. Aged two or three weeks, the young start doing 'press-ups' with their wing tips to prepare for the journey back to Africa, and fledge after another three to six weeks. They fly to Africa within days of fledging.

How to attract them The swift has suffered huge declines in recent years so needs all the help it can get, so erect nest boxes under the eaves of your house to encourage them to set up home.

HELP!

I've found a grounded swift. It can't fly.

Due to their long wings and short legs, all but the strongest swifts are unable to launch themselves into flight from the ground. So if a baby falls out of the nest it will perish unless given a helping hand.

What can I do? If it's an adult and you think it can fly, hold it in the palms of your hands and raise your hands high in the air. Make sure you're releasing the bird into the wind and choose a place where, if it comes straight back down, you can find it. If it's really thin, or a baby that's fallen before it's able to fly, it will need caring for before it can be released. Swifts are hard to care for, so need to be looked after by experts. Pick it up and pop it in a box with a lid on it so it can settle down, and contact your local bird group or society for help.

ABOVE *The scythe-shaped wings of the swift are easily seen from ground level.*

House martin (*Delichon urbicum*)

Like the swift, the house martin is a summer migrant from Africa that spends much of its time in the air and eats invertebrates on the wing. It's also likely to nest communally under the eaves of our houses. But, unlike swift nests, house martin nests are visible, constructed from mud on the outside of buildings.

The house martin is blue-black with a white underside that's visible from below, and has a forked tail. Unlike the swift it doesn't screech, but makes a repetitive, chattering sound.

Females lay up to two clutches of four or five eggs, which are incubated for 14–16 days. The young fledge after 19–25 days. Unlike swifts, which return to Africa as soon as the young have fledged, house martins can stay well into autumn. Like swallows, which belong in the same (Hirundinidae) family, they may gather on telephone wires before heading back to Africa.

How to attract them A patch of mud, which they'll use to make their nests, can lure them into your garden in dry spring weather while a pre-bought nest box or three fixed beneath the eaves of your home could entice a colony to move in.

BELOW *While the tail of the house martin is similar to the swift's, the prominent white underside of the house martin helps to tell them apart.*

Swallow (*Hirundo rustica*)

Like the swift and house martin, the swallow migrates from Africa every spring to breed, but it can be told apart from the swift and house martin by its long tail streamers. It can often be seen circling overhead in groups, or swooping low over the ground. Both male and female are metallic blue with whitish underparts and a reddish brown forehead, throat and chin. The male has longer tail streamers than the female.

Swallows are not specifically garden birds, and seem to prefer open pasture with access to water and quiet farm buildings. They feed on the wing, catching airborne spiders and insects. The male and female build the nest from mud and plant material, often in an out building such as a barn. Large flocks can often be seen perching on telephone wires in autumn before heading back to Africa.

The female lays up to two clutches of four or five eggs and incubates them for 14–16 days. Both parents feed the young, which fledge after 19–25 days.

The swallow is in decline, possibly due to climate change or a fall in the number of breeding sites.

How to attract them They're not really a garden bird but you can help them by growing a patch of long grass and digging a pond to boost insect activity. If you live in a rural area you might help them by providing a patch of mud in dry weather.

ABOVE *Look out for white underparts and tail streamers. Swallows also tend to fly closer to the ground than house martins and swifts.*

Robin (*Erithacus rubecula*)

One of the most recognisable garden birds, the robin is brown with big black eyes and an orange-red breast. It's also one of the birds we gardeners are most likely to come into contact with – dig over a patch of soil and you may be joined by a little red-breasted friend looking for worms.

The male and female have similar colouring but juveniles have a brown, speckled breast (they grow red feathers after about three months). It tends to feed on the ground, eating invertebrates such as worms and beetles.

Nests are made from grass, moss and leaves in thickets of ivy, tree hollows and open-fronted nest boxes. They may also be made on the ground. Nesting pairs raise up to three broods of four to five eggs per year, which are incubated for 13–14 days. The young fledge 13–14 days after hatching.

How to attract them Build a log pile to increase numbers of beetles and other invertebrates in your garden, and mulch the soil to increase worm activity.

Blackbird (*Turdus merula*)

The blackbird has one of the most beautiful songs of all garden birds: a rich, fluty call that often lasts throughout summer. Only the male is black; the female is a dull brown, often with paler streaks on her throat and breast. Juveniles are also brown, and young males don't develop a bright orange beak until the following year.

The blackbird eats worms and insects from lawns and borders. In winter, it eats windfall fruit and berries, and turns leaves over in search of grubs.

The nest is made using grass, twigs and mud. The female lays up to four smooth, bluish eggs with reddish-brown spots. Eggs are incubated for two weeks and fledglings leave the nest after a further two weeks. Nesting pairs can have as many as four broods per season.

How to attract them Make leaf piles or mulch borders with leaf mould, and leave windfall apples on the ground.

ABOVE *An adult male blackbird (identified by its orange beak) perches on a tree.* **LEFT** *A robin shelters in a tree. Note its big eyes, which enable it to see better than other bird species, meaning it can forage earlier in the day.*

Song thrush *(Turdus philomelos)*

To have a song thrush in the garden is a wonderful thing, not just for its beautiful song, but for its appetite for snails. It's smaller than the blackbird and less upright when standing. Adults are brown, with arrow-like markings on their golden-cream breast. It eats worms, insects, berries and snails. If you're lucky, you may see one using a stone in your garden as an anvil to open snail shells.

The female makes her nest in a tree or bush, using grass, twigs and earth, and a lining of smoothed mud and rotten wood, and lays up to four blue eggs with black spots. Eggs are incubated for 13–14 days and fledglings leave the nest roughly two weeks after hatching. Song thrushes tend to have up to three broods per season, but if there's plenty of food around, they may have as many as five.

How to attract them Keep an area of your lawn short, mulch borders and plant fruiting shrubs, such as holly.

ABOVE *The arrow-like markings are clearly visible on this singing song thrush.*

Fieldfare *(Turdus pilaris)*

The fieldfare is a large thrush, about the same size as a mistle thrush. The male and female are similar looking, mainly brown and grey with a creamy, streaked breast. It eats insects, worms and berries, and stands upright, moving with purposeful hops.

The cup-shaped nest is made in trees, from grass, moss and twigs, and lined with mud. The female lays up to two clutches of five to six eggs which she incubates for 11–14 days. The young leave the nest after 12–16 days.

Although there are a few breeding pairs in Orkney in Scotland, and its European breeding range includes France, Holland and Norway, we're most likely to come across fieldfares as winter migrants.

Large numbers migrate west from Scandinavia and roam the countryside in flocks. Only when berries are in short supply in rural areas, do they come into gardens.

How to attract them Grow plenty of berry-producing plants including hawthorn and cotoneaster, and leave halved apples and mealworms on the ground.

BELOW *Keep an eye out for large thrushes on your lawn in winter; they may be fieldfares.*

Long-tailed tit *(Aegithalos caudatus)*

The long-tailed tit is absolutely adorable, like a little flying badger. Small, fluffy and pinkish, with a long tail, adults gather in extended family groups in winter, egging each other on with a little 'deet-deet' to fly, in turn, from one tree to another. It's not a true tit, being in a separate genus, *Aegithalos*. It's predominantly an insect-eater, taking moth and butterfly eggs, bugs and small insects, but some have recently learned to use garden feeders.

The nest may take three weeks to build and is an elaborate ball of moss, spiders' webs, lichen, feathers and hair. The female lays between six and nine smooth, glossy white eggs with purple-red spots. Eggs are incubated for 14–16 days and the young fledge from 14–17 days. Family members that don't breed successfully often help those with large broods.

How to attract them Plant trees and dense, thorny bushes for them to shelter in and find food.

ABOVE *A long-tailed tit clings to a branch, which it may be scouring for tiny morsels such as moth eggs.* **RIGHT** *The blue crown, white face and yellow underbelly are clearly visible on this blue tit clinging on to a tree branch.*

Blue tit *(Cyanistes caeruleus)*

The blue tit is a gorgeous mix of blue, yellow, white and green. It eats insects, spiders and berries as well as peanuts, sunflower seeds and fat-based products from feeders. You might spot one picking insects, one by one, off plant stems or hanging upside down from tree branches. The male and female have the same colouring, but fledglings look like they've had a lemon wash – their feathers are duller and tinged with yellow.

Blue tits are common users of nest boxes. The female builds her nest from moss, wool, grass and hair, before laying between eight and ten smooth, white eggs with purple or brown spots. Breeding pairs tend to have just one brood a year, which they incubate for 12–16 days. The young fledge after 16–22 days.

How to attract them Install a nest box and plant deciduous trees or a hedge to boost numbers of insects, spiders and caterpillars.

Great tit *(Parus major)*

The great tit is bigger than the blue tit. It's grey-green and yellow, with a distinctive black stripe down the breast (this is more prominent in males, and males with the widest stripes are more dominant and also more attractive to females). Like blue tits, great tits favour invertebrates, particularly caterpillars, beetles and flies, and eat more tree seeds in autumn and winter. They take peanuts, sunflower seeds and fat-based products from garden feeders. In spring, adults feed caterpillars, spiders and insects to their young.

Great tits make their nests in holes in trees and nest boxes, using moss, grass, down, hair and feathers. The female lays up to two clutches of eggs per year, consisting of six to nine eggs per clutch. The white eggs are smooth and glossy with purplish-red spots. They're incubated for 12–16 days and the young fledge after 15–22 days.

How to attract them Install a nest box and plant as many deciduous trees as you can.

ABOVE *The large black bib of this adult male great tit suggest it is quite dominant and also popular among the ladies!* LEFT *The female great tit has a noticeably smaller bib.*

Goldfinch (*Carduelis carduelis*)

Golden brown with yellow, white and black wings and a bright red face, the goldfinch is one of the most colourful birds likely to visit your garden. Males and females are hard to tell apart but juveniles lack the colourful facial markings. It's mainly a seed-eater, known for eating niger and sunflower seed at the bird table, but it also eats seeds of teasel, thistles and dandelion, and occasionally insects.

Goldfinches often gather in small flocks so you may have a gang of them visiting your garden. You might hear them before you see them – they have a lovely twittering call.

In spring the female builds a cup-shaped nest with moss, grass and lichen, usually in a tree or shrub. She lays two or three clutches of around five eggs and incubates them for 12–13 days. The young are fed by both parents, before fledging after 14–15 days. Many migrate south as far as Spain in autumn.

How to attract them Leave seedheads on teasels and dandelions, and fill feeders with sunflower and niger seed.

Greenfinch (*Carduelis chloris*)

The greenfinch's wheezing song is unmistakable, sounding a bit like a tired, contented sigh. Only the male is green; the female is more of a dull brown, with green eye patches. Both have yellow-green edges to the wings. Adults eat mainly seeds but will also take berries and rosehips in winter. They feed insects and spiders to their young.

Greenfinches are unlikely to use nest boxes and often nest in small colonies in dense shrubs and conifer trees. The nest is made from twigs, grass, moss and hair. Nesting pairs usually have two broods per season, with the female laying four or five smooth, glossy white eggs with blackish markings. Eggs are incubated for 11–15 days and fledglings leave the nest some 13–16 days later.

How to attract them Fill feeders with sunflower hearts, and plant dense shrubs and hedges for them to nest in.

ABOVE *A greenfinch perches on a branch.* **LEFT** *A niger-seed feeder is one of the best ways to lure goldfinches to your garden.*

Chaffinch (Fringilla coelebs)

You're most likely to see chaffinches foraging on the ground for insects, or under the bird table for spilt sunflower seeds, but they will also visit hanging feeders. The male is chestnut brown with a distinctive pink underbelly and the female is more olive brown with a grey-brown belly. Both have two white bars on each wing, and a green rump.

The nest is made in trees and shrubs and is a beautiful cup of moss, grass and feathers bound with spiders' webs. It's lined with feathers and wool and then finished off with lichen and flakes of bark. The female usually lays one brood of four to five smooth, glossy, light-blue eggs with purple-brown blotches. Eggs are incubated for 11–13 days and the young leave the nest after 13–16 days.

How to attract them Provide lots of dense, shrubby cover and as many trees as you have space for.

ABOVE *The male bullfinch is easily identified by his pinky-red breast and stocky appearance.* **BELOW** *A male chaffinch waits patiently for the wildlife gardener to come and refill his feeder.*

Bullfinch (Pyrrhula pyrrhula)

The beauty of a bullfinch is enough to stop you in your tracks. A stocky, shy bird with a mournful call, it's most commonly found in the trees and dense undergrowth of woodland, although it's increasingly coming into gardens, particularly rural gardens with plenty of tree cover.

The colourful male with his pinky-red breast is often seen with his less colourful mate, or in small family groups.

The bullfinch eats the flower buds of fruit trees and was once considered a pest of orchards. It also eats seeds of plants such as nettle, bramble, ash, birch and honesty, as well as berries, and preys on insects to feed its young and may visit hanging feeders in gardens.

The nest is a loose platform of twigs, moss, lichens and plant roots, built by the female. She lays up to three clutches of four to five eggs and incubates them for 12–14 days. Both parents feed the young, which fledge after 14–16 days.

How to attract them Grow plenty of trees, including fruiting ones (although you may not appreciate what they do to your fruit blossom).

House sparrow (*Passer domesticus*)

The house sparrow is declining in Europe. This is possibly due to loss of nesting sites, changes in agriculture and a lack of insects, particularly aphids.

The male has a grey crown and black stripes around the eyes and on the bib (the area just below the beak). The paler female lacks the grey crown, black bib and eye stripe, and has a straw-coloured stripe behind the eye instead. Adults eat seeds as well as insects, and feed insects to their young.

The house sparrow lives in colonies in holes in buildings, or nest boxes. The nest is made with leaves, grass and even rubbish. Nesting pairs can have up to five broods of four to five, speckled white eggs per year, which are incubated for 11–14 days. Fledglings emerge after 11–19 days.

How to attract them Boost insect numbers by letting an area of grass grow long, planting a deciduous tree or hedge and making a log pile, and please tolerate a few aphids!

Waxwing (*Bombycilla garrulus*)

The waxwing is unmistakable. Roughly the size of a starling, it has a distinctive Mohican-like crest, a black throat and eye mask, yellow and grey wings and a yellow-tipped tail.

For most of the year it lives in the taiga forests of Scandinavia and Russia, feeding on insects, flower buds and berries. Migrating south for winter, large numbers can sometimes arrive in Britain and France when berries are in short supply back home.

The female builds the nest using twigs, grass and lichen, and lines it with grass, moss and pine needles. She lays four to six eggs, which she incubates herself for around two weeks, but both adults feed the young once they've hatched. The young fledge after 15–17 days.

How to attract them You'll only see them in winter, so plant lots of berry-producing shrubs, especially rowan, guelder rose, hawthorn and cotoneaster. Leaving halved apples on the ground or in your hedge may also attract them.

ABOVE *A waxwing perches on the branch of one of its favourite berrying plants – the guelder rose.* **RIGHT** *Note the grey crown and black stripes around the eye and bib of this male house sparrow.*

Blackcap (*Sylvia atricapilla*)

A greyish warbler more commonly seen in gardens (especially those with a lot of tree and shrub cover). Only the male has a black cap; the female's is chestnut brown. In spring and summer it eats caterpillars, flies and spiders, and switches to fruit in winter. It's also increasingly seen at garden bird tables.

In spring, the female builds a fragile nest of moss and grass in a nettle bed or bramble. She lays up to two clutches of four or five eggs, which both adults incubate for 11–12 days. The young usually fledge after 11–12 days.

You might see blackcaps in your garden all year round, but they're unlikely to be the same birds. Breeding pairs from Britain and Western Europe tend to fly south to Iberia and northern Africa for winter, but in recent years some pairs from Germany, Belgium and Holland have been spending winter in Britain instead. It's thought that the milder British winters and an abundance of supplementary food provided by British gardeners has led to the change in behaviour. Blackcaps wintering in Britain are at an advantage to those that winter in Iberia and Africa, as they are closer to, and are therefore the first to arrive at the breeding grounds.

How to attract them Grow plenty of trees and shrubs for breeding pairs in spring and summer, and keep feeders well stocked in winter.

Wren (*Troglodytes troglodytes*)

Small, brown and fidgety, with a cocked tail, the wren dashes about eating spiders and insects, probing crevices with its long, thin beak. It can suffer in winter when food is in short supply, and large numbers may squeeze into bird boxes, for warmth.

In spring, the male makes several nests of leaves, moss and grass for the female to choose from. Once the female has picked her favourite, she decorates it with feathers. She then lays five to six smooth, glossy white eggs with reddish spots, which she incubates for 13–18 days. Wrens can have two broods per year, but the male may have more than one female in his territory (well, if he's made all those nests…). Fledglings emerge after 14–19 days.

How to attract them Provide lots of potential nesting sites for males to woo a female or three, and make a log pile.

ABOVE *A male blackcap rests on a tree branch.* **BELOW** *A wren perches on a garden fence. Note its cocked tail and alert stance.*

Mammals

You'll find mammals anywhere in the garden, including under the shed or among piles of logs or leaves, high up in trees or low down in long grass. As long as they can enter and exit your garden easily, and have space to nest, shelter and feed, they'll be quite at home. Common species include squirrels, hedgehogs and wood mice, but you may also see badgers, bats and foxes. For some gardeners, rabbits, deer and moles are seen as pests, but others welcome them with open arms. Few gardeners are hospitable to rats.

Identifying most mammals is easy. It's simple telling a fox apart from a badger or a rabbit apart from a hedgehog, but learning the difference between a vole and a wood mouse is more difficult. If you have bats flying over your garden, you may want to invest in a bat detector to help you identify your pipistrelle from your Daubenton's.

Look out for visible tracks, or signs. All mammals leave poo, trapped fur, footprints or the remains of food, so with a bit of practice you'll be able to work out what's visiting.

HELP!

How can I stop my cat from killing local wildlife?

Cats kill millions of small mammals and birds every year, and they also like to catch, play with and sometimes kill bats and frogs.

What can I do? Fix a collar and bell to your cat so birds and small mammals can hear it coming. Between mid-spring and mid-autumn, when bird and mammal activity is at its peak, bring your cat indoors before sunset and keep it in until an hour after sunset (all night if possible); this is especially important in summer, when bats are caring for their young.

OPPOSITE *A grey squirrel rests in a rowan tree in autumn, having built its drey higher up out of danger.*

Ten things to do for mammals

❶ Build log and leaf piles (see pages 20 and 22).
❷ Make access holes at the bottom of your fences (see page 13).
❸ Grow nectar-rich plants, to attract insects (see page 36).
❹ Build bonfires just before you light them, to avoid inadvertently setting fire to hibernating creatures.
❺ Keep pea netting off the ground, so animals can't get tangled up in it.
❻ Let a patch of grass grow long to encourage insect activity and therefore provide more food for bats.

❼ Compost waste (see page 18) to provide food and shelter for nesting and hibernating mammals.
❽ Avoid using slug pellets, as they may be eaten and can cause harm.
❾ Plant a hedge and include species like hazel (*Corylus avellana*) and honeysuckle (*Lonicera periclymenum*) to provide food in autumn for small mammals.
❿ Dig a pond (see page 60) or make a bog garden to provide drinking water and also increase insect activity, resulting in more food for bats and other insect-eaters.

Fox (*Vulpes vulpes*)

The red fox is all pointy face, burnt orange coat, white chest and big, bushy tail. It's typically found in rural areas, but the so-called 'urban fox' has recently adapted to live in towns and cities – you might find a family living under your shed.

Foxes emerge at dusk to forage on anything from insects, earthworms, fruit and berries, to birds, small mammals and carrion. They will eat scraps left by humans and may rummage through your bins to access food you've thrown away.

Mating takes place in late winter. The mating call can be quite terrifying if you've not heard it before – a sort of wild shriek. Around five cubs are born in spring.

How to attract them Ensure they can access your garden. If you'd rather deter them, block entrance holes to potential nesting sites and if you live in an urban area, make sure your bins have tight-fitting lids and cannot be knocked over.

HELP!

There are two foxes stuck together – they've been there for hours!

Don't worry, this is perfectly normal, if perhaps a little frustrating for the foxes. There can be a bit of swelling after mating, causing the dog fox and vixen to lock together, known as a 'tie'. Unable to dismount, the male swings his back leg over the vixen and they wait, back to back, for the swelling to go down.

What can I do? Just leave them to it, and try to stay out of the garden until they've vacated.

Badger (*Meles meles*)

The badger is short and stocky, with silvery-grey fur and black-and-white facial markings. It lives mostly in woodland in family groups, occupying underground setts in territories that are marked by partially buried 'latrines'. Nocturnal creatures, badgers emerge at dusk and spend the night foraging for food. Breeding takes place all year round and up to six cubs are born per litter.

The badger's diet consists mainly of earthworms, but they may also eat frogs, rodents, hedgehogs, birds, eggs, lizards, insects, bulbs, seeds and berries. In dry summers, worms retreat far below the soil's surface, so badgers may dig up bumblebee and wasp nests to eat. They're also partial to digging up lawns to eat chafer grubs.

How to attract them Ensure they can access your garden and leave food out for them. If you'd rather deter them, consult your local badger group for advice.

Badgers keep digging up my lawn!

Badgers eat worms and insect larvae, and can dig up lawns looking for leatherjackets and chafer grubs. It's not a problem if they're just eating worms, which they merely suck out of the ground, but they use their paws to dig out grubs, leaving big, muddy patches in the sward. Digging activity and damage tend to peak in autumn. Some gardeners tolerate this as an aesthetic compromise for having badgers in the garden; others would rather have a nice lawn.

What can I do? The easiest way to solve the problem is to scatter peanuts over the area, which the badgers will eat instead of digging for grubs (it's also lovely to watch). But if this is a huge problem and you really want a long-term solution, you need to remove the larvae that attract the badgers. You can deter crane flies and chafers from laying eggs by regularly mowing, removing moss and aerating the lawn. You can also apply nematodes, which safely kill the grubs without harming other wildlife.

OPPOSITE ABOVE *Urban foxes like this one may be seen during the day.*
OPPOSITE BELOW *This old log is probably full of grubs – perfect for badgers.*

Rabbit *(Oryctolagus cuniculus)*

Native to the Mediterranean, the rabbit is now a valuable part of our fauna as many species, including badgers, buzzards and stoats, rely on rabbits for food. Rabbits are rarely welcome in gardens, as they eat fruit and vegetables and can also strip bark from young trees.

They have brown fur, a pale belly and long ears, and live in an underground network of burrows and bolt-holes, known as a warren. Breeding takes place in spring and summer; the female builds a nest from grass, which she lines with soft fur from her belly, and gives birth to litters of up to seven kittens.

How to attract them It's probably not a great idea to encourage rabbits, but if they're already in your garden, arm yourself with some tree guards and a fruit and vegetable cage (60cm high and buried 5cm under the soil) and try to learn to live with them.

ABOVE *If rabbits only stuck to grass, they'd be much more popular with gardeners.*

Red squirrel (*Sciurus vulgaris*),
Grey squirrel (*Sciurus carolinensis*)

You may have either the native red or the introduced grey in your garden. Both have similar habits, but the grey has displaced the red over much of the British Isles and parts of Italy.

The grey squirrel is native to North America and carries squirrel pox, which can be fatal to reds. Silvery grey with a large fluffy tail, it's bigger than the red, which is reddish brown with a white belly, bushy tail and furry ears. Both eat tree seeds, flower buds and bulbs, shoots and fungi, but the grey is better at finding food.

Squirrel nests (dreys) are a messy ball of twigs made in holes in trees or where branches fork. Breeding starts in late winter, and females have up to two litters of around four kittens each year.

How to attract them Feed reds to help them breed successfully (see page 55). You may also want to feed greys, but it's virtually impossible to deter them!

Weasel (*Mustela nivalis*), Stoat (*Mustela erminea*)

Weasels and stoats are common and widespread in Europe, although the weasel is absent from Ireland. The stoat is larger than the weasel and has a longer tail with a black tip. Both species eat mice, voles and birds and their eggs, but stoats also take larger prey, such as rabbits.

Males and females establish separate territories, making a series of dens from the former nests of prey, which may be lined with the fur of the previous tenant. Mating takes place in late spring and early summer, but pregnancy is delayed in stoats until the following spring. Litters of up to 12 stoats and six weasels are born. After 12 weeks, the kits (the young) are ready to face the world on their own.

How to attract them If you live in a rural area, ensure your garden has a good supply of their favourite food.

ABOVE *The black tail tip identifies the stoat (above) from the weasel (below).* **BELOW** *This red squirrel is collecting leaves to take to its drey. It doesn't hibernate, but spends most of its time in the drey in winter, so the more leaves it can collect, the cosier the drey.*

OPPOSITE *A hedgehog forages for beetles and slugs among fallen leaves.*

HELP!

I've disturbed a hedgehog's nest

If a nest has been disturbed, some hedgehog mothers will abandon or kill their young, while others may just move them to a new location, or even settle back down if the nest hasn't been disturbed too much.

What can I do? Try to replace as much nesting material as you can and don't disturb the nest again. Place a twig or leaf over the entrance, which the mother will have to brush aside, so you can tell if she is still making regular trips to and from the nest. It's also a good idea to pop a dish each of water and canned meat-based dog or cat food outside, so she doesn't have to travel far in order to replace energy to suckle her young. If the mum doesn't appear to be returning to the nest, or if you hear squeaking from within, then the hoglets need to be rescued. Call your local hedgehog carer for advice (see page 143 for details).

Hedgehog *(Erinaceus europaeus)*

The hedgehog is almost entirely covered in spines, although the belly and chest are covered in a coarse brown fur, which is visible as a sort of underskirt. They can be quite noisy little things, often grunting and snuffling like small, prickly pigs.

Adults nest in compost bins, under sheds, in leaf piles and clumps of ornamental grass. They also hibernate in these places, typically between late autumn and early spring. Nocturnal, they travel long distances to mate and find food, which includes caterpillars and beetles, earthworms, leatherjackets, earwigs and slugs. They also eat food that we leave out for them (see page 54).

Mating takes place in spring and summer, and up to five young are born per litter between early summer and autumn.

How to attract them Plant a hedge and make leaf piles for them to nest in, and ensure they can enter and exit your garden easily.

HELP!

I've just seen a hedgehog out during the day. I thought they were nocturnal?

Hedgehogs are primarily nocturnal, but nesting mothers may be seen out during the day in spring and summer, gathering materials or even moving their babies to a more suitable nesting site. However, if you see a hedgehog lying down during the day, it could be an orphaned baby or injured, poisoned or just cold.

A hedgehog foraging during the day in autumn is likely to be a late-born baby that hasn't gained enough weight in order to survive hibernation. As each autumn day passes, natural food sources, such as caterpillars and slugs, are in ever-decreasing supply, so the hedgehog's chances of survival are slim. If it's particularly small, or lying down or staggering about, it will need immediate help.

What can I do? Take it in and keep it warm. Pop it on a hot-water bottle wrapped in a towel, place it in a high-sided box lined with newspaper, and then place another towel over the hedgehog to make it feel secure. Ensure the bottle is kept warm. Offer it some water and meat-based dog or cat food. If the hedgehog doesn't take the food, or if it seems injured, call your local hedgehog carer or hedgehog society for advice (see page 143 for details).

Mole *(Talpa europaea)*

The mole is about the same size as the hedgehog, with short, black, velvety fur. It has squinty little eyes, a whiskery pink snout and giant, spade-like front feet. It spends almost all of its life underground. Mostly solitary, adults meet up in spring to mate, and litters contain three or four young.

Moles tend not to be loved by gardeners, as they can cause havoc to veg plots, ornamental displays and lawns. However, they can also be beneficial to the gardener, feeding on insect larvae such as cockchafer grubs and carrot fly as well as earthworms. Their tunnels also help to aerate and break down compacted soils.

They're present over most of Europe, with the noticeable exception of Ireland, and are unlikely to visit gardens in urban or suburban areas.

How to attract them Perhaps just tolerate them, rather than attract them. They're difficult to deter so grit your teeth and use the soil from molehills as a medium in which to sow seeds.

Bank vole *(Myodes glareolus)*, Field vole *(Microtus agrestis)*

Voles have a thick coat, furry ears, a short tail and a rounded, whiskery snout. The most common garden visitor is the chestnut-coloured bank vole, which eats fruit, nuts, snails and small insects. Bank voles live at the base of hedges and beneath shrubs.

The field vole inhabits larger, rural gardens where lawns are left unmown. Its whole life revolves around grass, which it eats, shelters and nests in. It spends most of its time hiding from predators, but look out for well-worn paths in long grass, piles of cut grass and greenish (grassy!) droppings.

Both species breed between early spring and early winter, having up to six litters of four or five young per year. Field voles tend to nest above ground (in grass), while bank voles nest below ground in burrows.

How to attract them Let an area of grass grow long, create patches of dense vegetation and make a log pile.

ABOVE *A bank vole can be identified by its chesnut-coloured fur, small ears and rounded, whiskery snout.* **BELOW** *A mole pokes its head out of the ground; its huge front feet explain why it's so good at digging.*

OPPOSITE ABOVE *The big eyes and ears are characteristic of a wood mouse.* **OPPOSITE BELOW** *A pipistrelle bat flies at night.*

Wood mouse *(Apodemus sylvaticus)*

The wood mouse can be told apart from the house mouse by its sandy brown coat, long tail, big ears and big eyes; the house mouse (*Mus musculus*) is grey, with a shorter tail and smaller eyes and ears.

The wood mouse eats mostly seeds and fruit, but also insects and small snails. Nests are made in underground burrows, sheds and compost heaps, and are lined with leaves, moss and grass. The female gives birth to up to three litters of around nine babies per year, and the young are ready to reproduce within three weeks. Their lifespan can be as little as three months, and owls, kestrels, foxes, badgers, weasels and cats all eat them. The wood mouse is also firmly entrenched in the wider garden ecosystem: old burrows are used by nesting bumblebees and other species may hibernate in them.

How to attract them Provide dense vegetation and access to your compost bin.

Bats

Bats are the only flying mammals. They can see but 'echolocate' to fly and feed at night, sending out shouts and listening to the returning echoes to create a 'sound picture' of what's around them. These shouts are inaudible to humans, but you can hear them using a bat detector, which can help to identify them.

Bats eat beetles, moths and flies, including mosquitoes and midges. Some tropical species also pollinate plants. The most likely species to visit your garden are pipistrelles, which have a fast, jerky flight when hunting insects.

Bats don't make nests, but roost in a number of places, including trees and canal bridges. They use different roosts for different purposes, generally preferring warm roosts in summer and cold ones in winter.

How to attract them Grow deciduous trees, where insects can gather, dig a pond and grow plenty of plants for pollinators, such as moths, which large bats eat.

HELP!

I've found a bat on the ground, does it need help?

Probably, yes. Bats come to ground when they're exhausted and starving – often during cold, wet summers, when insects are in short supply.

What can I do? Use a glove or cloth to put the bat in a box with kitchen paper in the bottom, a small soft cloth to make it feel secure and a tin lid of water. Phone the Bat Conservation Trust Helpline for details of your nearest bat carer (see page 143).

Amphibians and reptiles

Amphibians and reptiles are gorgeous-looking things, like creatures from a forgotten time. Many gardens are home to common frogs, toads and smooth newts, but you may also encourage slow worms, common lizards and even grass snakes to visit, depending on where you live.

Identifying them can be tricky, at first. Frogs are often mistaken for toads, smooth and palmate newts look virtually identical, and slow worms may be mistaken for snakes. But don't let this put you off! With a little practice, you'll soon be able to tell a common lizard from a smooth newt, a slow worm from a grass snake, and a frog from a toad.

Look out for mating frogs, toads and newts in spring, and grass snakes and common lizards basking in sunshine.

LEFT *Note the dry, warty skin of this toad which enables it to spend long periods of time away from water.* **OPPOSITE** *A rare glimpse of a smooth newt as it exits a pond.*

Ten things to do for amphibians

❶ Dig a pond with gentle sloping sides and a deeper area for overwintering frogs, and plenty of aquatic plants (see page 60).

❷ Create a large, open compost heap (see page 18).

❸ Make a log pile (see page 22).

❹ Let an area of grass grow long, particularly around your pond (see page 24).

❺ Build a dry-stone wall or mini-cairn (see page 23).

❻ Create dense areas of vegetation in your borders.

❼ Sweep fallen leaves under your hedge or place them in a purpose-built wire cage (see page 20).

❽ Avoid killing slugs and snails, which amphibians eat.

❾ Create refuges for slow worms by laying a square of carpet over long grass in a sunny spot.

❿ Make a hibernaculum for amphibians and their prey to shelter in during the winter months (see page 20).

HELP!

What's wrong with my frogs?

Since the 1980s, a devastating virus called ranavirus has swept through the UK, killing frogs and other amphibians, as well as reptiles. The virus is most noticeable in mid-summer. Frogs display a range of symptoms, from a reddening of the skin (the virus is sometimes called 'red leg'), to ulcers, haemorrhaging, drowsiness, emaciation and eye problems. Most people simply just find a large number of dead frogs in their garden.

What can I do? There's no cure at the moment, but the virus does pass through frog populations and they can recover after an outbreak. Research suggests that some frogs are resistant to the disease. Avoid spreading it by digging a deep hole to bury the bodies.

Common frog *(Rana temporaria)*

No garden should be without the common frog, with its big eyes, shiny wet skin and appetite for slugs and snails.

Males tend to be smaller than females, especially when females develop spawn. In spring, males develop a single vocal sac, which looks like a large double chin, and they can also take on a bluish tinge.

Fertilisation is external. Males grasp onto females tightly (known as amplexus) and spawn is laid in clumps. Tadpoles start off by eating algae, before developing a taste for the occasional bit of dead animal when their legs start to grow. Most froglets have left the pond by late summer, but won't be sexually active for two to three years.

In autumn, juvenile and female frogs overwinter in ditches, log and leaf piles, while many males head to the muddy bottom of ponds.

How to attract them Dig a pond and make a log pile.

ABOVE LEFT AND ABOVE *Common frogs can be identified by their pointed nose, shiny wet skin and black marks around the eyes.*

HELP!

I've disturbed a hibernating toad/frog

Don't worry, it will probably be fine. Frogs and toads hibernate in compost bins, log piles, ditches and the muddy depths of ponds. Disturbing them can expose them to predators, but they should be fine if they're quickly moved back to a similar, sheltered environment.

What can I do? Move the frog or toad to a similar spot, like a compost heap or log pile. Don't put it in the pond.

Common toad (*Bufo bufo*)

The common toad has a round face and brown, warty skin, which allows it to go for long periods away from water. It also has a swollen poison gland behind each eye, which secretes a slightly toxic substance to deter predators. It eats snails, slugs, ants, beetles and spiders.

Adults return to the pond they were spawned in, and often make annual pilgrimages to ancestral mating grounds in spring. But this doesn't mean they won't use your garden pond. In every local population there are often a few that break away and try something new.

Mating is similar to that of frogs, usually taking place a couple of weeks later. Spawn is laid in strings and wrapped around submerged plant stems. Toadlets and adults spend the winter buried in mud, under compost heaps or among dead wood such as log piles.

The common toad is widespread over most of Europe except for Ireland and northern Scandinavia.

How to attract them Dig a large, deep pond and make log and leaf piles for them to shelter in and forage for food.

Smooth newt (*Lissotriton vulgaris*)

The smooth newt is brown with a spotty yellow-orange belly. During the breeding season the male develops a wavy crest. Breeding takes place throughout spring, with males appearing to 'dance' on the bottom of the pond. When a male has convinced a female to mate with him, he leaves his sperm in a packet called a spermatophore at the bottom of the pond, and she picks it up and fertilises herself internally. She then lays eggs, individually wrapping them in the leaves of plants such as water forget-me-not (*Myosotis scorpioides*).

Newt larvae have external feathery gills behind their head. They leave the pond in late summer, when they're called newtlets or 'efts', and spend autumn and winter sheltering under rocks or logs, or in compost heaps.

How to attract them Grow pond plants in your pond and make piles of stones, leaf litter and logs for them to take shelter.

ABOVE *The warty skin and more rounded appearance of toads identifies them from frogs.* **RIGHT** *A smooth newt looks for shelter on land.*

Grass snake (*Natrix natrix*)

Non-venomous, the worst a grass snake can do to you is release a foul-smelling liquid, or musk, if you pick it up (in actual fact, it doesn't smell too bad – rather like wild garlic). It has a distinctive yellow collar around the neck, a scaly, olive-green body and a black, forked tongue.

Females tend to be longer than males (they can grow to 1.2m, while males reach only 1m), although most you see will be quite small. Breeding takes place in late spring, and eggs are laid in early summer in compost heaps and other warm piles of vegetation. Grass snakes overwinter in compost heaps, log piles and beneath tree roots.

Baby grass snakes eat tadpoles and juvenile amphibians, moving on to adult frogs, toads, newts and occasionally goldfish as they mature.

The grass snake is common and widespread over most of Europe except for Ireland and northern Scandinavia.

How to attract them Dig a pond and build a large, open compost heap for them to breed in.

Great crested newt (*Triturus cristatus*)

This declining newt is unlikely to visit your garden unless there's a population living nearby. The large adults have almost-black, warty skin and a spotted yellow-orange belly; males develop a jagged crest and a white tail stripe during the breeding season.

Adults tend to live on land, although some may stay in ponds to feed after breeding. They seem to prefer larger ponds and ditches, but may visit smaller garden ponds. They have an elaborate courtship routine in which males drive pheromones towards females with their tails. Females lay eggs in the leaves of pond plants. Newtlets emerge from ponds between late summer and mid-autumn, and hibernation takes place on land.

How to attract them Tell someone from your local Amphibian and Reptile Group if you have them in your garden. Great crested newts are protected by UK and European law, so you need a licence to disturb them.

ABOVE *The great crested newt is much larger than the smooth newt.*
BELOW *A grass snake travels through long grass.*

Slow worm (*Anguis fragilis*)

The slow worm is commonly mistaken for a snake, but is actually a legless lizard. Unlike snakes, it has eyelids, and it can shed its tail to escape predators. Brown, shiny and almost iridescent, slow worms often gather in large groups, resembling a big clump of spaghetti drizzled with olive oil. Males have a greyish tint and females have dark sides. Babies are thin with gold or silver sides.

Slow worms eat slugs, snails, woodlice, earthworms and insects. Compost bins provide the perfect, warm conditions for them, but they also take refuge under log piles and strips of corrugated iron placed in a sunny, secluded spot.

Breeding takes place in late spring. Females incubate their eggs internally and give birth to around eight live young in late summer.

The slow worm is common and widespread over most of Europe except for Ireland, southern Spain and northern Scandinavia.

How to attract them Provide access to your compost bin and make a log pile. A strip of corrugated iron laid over long grass makes an ideal slow worm refugium (place to take refuge).

ABOVE *A slow worm retreats to the safety of long grass.* **RIGHT** *If common lizards are living nearby, there's no reason why they shouldn't come into your garden if you provide shelter, food and basking sites such as wood.*

Common lizard (*Zootoca vivipara*)

Small and fast moving, the common lizard is more likely to turn up in rural gardens than urban ones. It has scaly, chequered skin, and individuals range in colour from dark green to grey-brown. The young are much darker than the adults – some are almost black. It eats flies, grasshoppers, ants and spiders, and can lose its tail to escape from predators.

Breeding takes place from mid- to late spring. The eggs are incubated internally, and up to 11 young are born in mid-summer.

You may spot several lizards at a time, basking on wood and stone in spring and autumn. Individuals return regularly to their favourite sites. They disappear in late autumn, hibernating in crevices and abandoned burrows.

How to attract them Make a log pile in a sunny spot, which they may use for basking, and let a patch of grass grow long so they can hunt for prey.

Bees and wasps

ABOVE *A solitary bee gorges on flowering currant in spring.*
OPPOSITE *A common carder bumblebee feeds on knapweed.*

Nearly all gardens have a range of bees passing through, from fluffy fat bumbles to little zippy things that never stay still for long enough for you to see what they are. Gardens are fantastic resources for bees, especially in early spring and late autumn, when wild sources of nectar and pollen can be in short supply. Most bees are harmless, although honeybee workers can be aggressive if they perceive a threat to their colony. Bumblebees and solitary bees rarely, if ever, sting.

Wasps are also well catered for in our gardens. As well as social species, which include the much-maligned common wasp (*Vespula vulgaris*), there are lesser-known solitary wasps. Many are predatory and do a great job of controlling caterpillars and aphids. Most of them go unnoticed and, like bees, rarely sting. However, in late summer, common wasp workers can become aggressive and can irritate during summer picnics. This lasts for only a couple of weeks; for the rest of the year, they are some of the best pest controllers you can attract to your garden.

Ten things to do for bees and wasps

❶ Grow a wide range of flowering plants from early spring to late autumn (see page 36).

❷ Let an area of grass grow long but also keep areas short – especially if solitary bees are already nesting there.

❸ Provide access to your compost heap (see page 18).

❹ Make log, stick and leaf piles which bumblebees may nest or hibernate in (see pages 20–22).

❺ Make a solitary bee hotel (see page 29).

❻ Leave patches of bare earth in sunny locations, for ground-nesting solitary bees.

❼ Provide a source of water (such as a bird bath with a few stones in) for honeybees and wasps.

❽ Grow a variety of caterpillar food-plants, as food for wasps (see page 42).

❾ Leave a pile of grass clippings in a corner which bumblebees may nest or hibernate in (see page 31).

❿ Provide a source of untreated wood, such as a fence post, shed or bird box, for social wasps. The queen and workers rasp the wood and take it back to the nest as pulp, which they use to build their intricate paper nests.

Bumblebees

Bumblebees are furry and often stripy. Most have black-and-yellow stripes with a white tail, but some have a gingery or mostly black coat. Many can be identified by the colour of their tails. They live in colonies in holes in the ground, tussocky grass or compost bins. Workers are always female and can often be identified by the little baskets of pollen they carry on their hind legs. Males often have a bit of facial hair, or 'moustache'.

Of the 53 European species, just 25 are found in the UK, and around 22 in Holland, 30 in Germany and 35 in France. While some bumblebees are already extinct, other species hang by a thread in small pockets of flower-rich grassland. Only around eight, plus one or two cuckoo bumblebees (which prey on social species), are likely to visit your garden.

Lifecycle Colonies are annual. The large queen emerges from hibernation in spring and starts a nest. She then spends her time laying eggs while her workers gather nectar and pollen for the grubs. In summer, she produces males and daughter queens, which mate, before the males die and the daughter queens find somewhere to hibernate, ready to start a new nest in spring. The original queen and her workers die.

Red-tailed bumblebee (*Bombus lapidarius*)

A gorgeous bee: velvet black with an orangey-red tail. The queens can be quite large, but the size of workers varies. Nests are established in spring. Males can be distinguished by a thin, lemon-yellow band on the thorax and a yellow 'moustache'. Workers have a short tongue and visit a wide range of flowers, but seem to prefer yellow ones. The red-tailed bumblebee may nest underground in old mouse holes or in wall cavities (I once found a nest in an old duvet that had been slung out.)

How to attract them Grow yellow flowers, especially bird's-foot trefoil (*Lotus corniculatus*).

Common carder bumblebee (*Bombus pascuorum*)

Little and ginger, the common carder typically nests in tussocky grass, compost bins and piles of grass clippings. The bees collect moss and 'card' it together like a cardigan to cover the nest. Workers vary in size and can be so small they resemble honeybees. They have a medium to long tongue, so feed on plants with long flower tubes like honeysuckle (*Lonicera*), foxgloves (*Digitalis*) and white dead-nettle (*Lamium album*).

All of this bobbing in and out of flowers can make the workers lose a lot of hair, and you may see one with a triangular-shaped bald patch on its thorax. They're also susceptible to being bleached by the sun, so can look quite raggedy by autumn. Common carder nests seem to go on and on; in milder areas, it's not unusual to find workers still on the wing in late autumn.

How to attract them Leave a patch of grass to grow long and tussocky. Grow flowers with long flower tubes.

OPPOSITE ABOVE *A red-tailed bumblebee feasts on bird's-foot trefoil.* **OPPOSITE BELOW** *Knapweed makes the perfect landing pad for this common carder.* **BELOW** *A large buff-tailed queen replenishes her reserves on perennial wallflower.* **RIGHT** *The pointed end of this cuckoo is obvious.*

Buff-tailed bumblebee *(Bombus terrestris)*

A large, widespread and robust bumblebee. The enormous queens are often the first to emerge in spring, sometimes as early as late winter. A very small number may even establish winter colonies and forage on winter-flowering shrubs such as the Oregon grape (*Mahonia aquifolium*). Nests are usually made underground.

They are mostly black, with a dark yellow band on the thorax and one on the abdomen; only the queen has an obvious buff-coloured tail (this can occasionally be orange-red). The short-tongued workers visit almost any type of flower where they can access nectar and pollen, and may even pierce holes in flowers with long flower tubes in order to reach the nectar (if you've ever seen holes in the top of your broad bean flowers, that's why). Queens may also drink honeydew – the sugary substance excreted by aphids.

How to attract them Grow winter-flowering plants and provide access to your compost bin.

Cuckoo bumblebees

Cuckoo bumblebees take over the nests of other bumblebees. There are no queens or workers, just males and females. Most species have specific hosts, which they have evolved to resemble. They emerge from hibernation later than their hosts, giving the host queen time to get a nest established.

Unlike bumblebee queens and workers, cuckoos have no pollen baskets, because they feed only themselves. They're larger and less hairy than bumblebees, and have a very pointed abdomen tip.

On finding a nest, the female may wait outside for a few days to take on its scent in order to enter unnoticed. She then goes in, kills the queen and lays her own eggs, which the existing workers feed.

How to attract them Provide good nesting conditions for bumblebees.

Honeybees

Honeybees range in colour from orange to almost black and tend to live in large hives owned by beekeepers, but they occasionally start a new colony on their own – often in a tree. There's just one species of honeybee, but lots of subspecies and races within the genus, often depending on where they originated from.

Lifecycle Social, like bumblebees, but colonies can reach up to 40,000 workers and last for years. In spring, the original queen and thousands of workers may 'swarm' to start a new colony elsewhere, and daughter queens may also set off with a few hundred workers to establish colonies of their own. Honeybees are at their most docile when swarming, and are usually collected by beekeepers around this time.

Honeybee (*Apis mellifera*)

The honeybee is small and slender. It has less body hair than bumblebees – typically a hairy thorax, with fewer hairs on the abdomen. Workers can vary in colour, with some being quite orange and others almost black. It's a generalist feeder with a short tongue, so can visit a range of open, single flowers. Like bumblebees, honeybee workers collect pollen in 'baskets' on their hind legs, and drink nectar. When they return to the colony, they regurgitate the nectar and comb the pollen off their legs. This is mixed together to make honey, which is used to feed the grubs. (Bumblebee 'honey' is more watery than the stuff produced by honeybees. This is because the honeybee workers flap their wings to evaporate excess water from the mixture, whereas bumblebees don't.)

How to attract them Grow a variety of plants with nectar- and pollen-rich flowers.

Solitary bees

These can look like anything from bumblebees and honeybees to wasps. Common species include red mason bees and leafcutter bees, and look out for the hairy-footed flower bee (*Anthophora plumipes*) in early spring.

Lifecycle Solitary bees don't live in colonies, (although many species nest communally, giving the appearance of a colony), but lay eggs in individual cells, which they leave with a parcel of pollen and nectar for the emerging grub to eat. Some burrow in the ground, others lay eggs in hollow plant stems or even holes in walls. Once grown, the grubs pupate into adults and overwinter in the nest, before emerging at exactly the right time the following year, to mate and start the whole process all over again. Many solitary bees are loyal to a particular nesting site, so the same family of bees may have been nesting in your wall, lawn or borders for years.

LEFT *Honeybee.* **OPPOSITE ABOVE** *Leafcutter bee.* **OPPOSITE RIGHT** *Nomada bee.* **OPPOSITE BELOW** *Red mason bee.*

Leafcutter bees
(Megachile)

Solitary, but prone to nesting communally, leafcutters are easy to spot due to their habit of cutting semi-circular pieces out of rose and wisteria leaves and carrying them to their nests. They also have a rather comical tendency of lifting up their abdomen when feeding.

There are several species, which superficially look similar to honeybees, but they have a patch of orange hairs on the base of their abdomen (called scopa), on which they collect pollen.

Leafcutters nest in hollow plant stems and dead wood, and readily use solitary bee hotels. Compared to honeybees and bumblebees, leafcutters are on the wing for only a relatively short time, typically between early and late summer.

How to attract them Make a solitary bee box (see page 29), and grow roses and wisteria.

Nomada bees (Nomada)

If you have ground-nesting solitary bees in your garden, take a closer look at the nest burrows and you may see small, wasp-like bees flying around, too. These are the beautiful nomada bees, which are kleptoparasites (food stealers) of solitary bees in the Andrena genus.

Female nomada bees lay their eggs in the nest created by the host bee for their own young. The host makes a cell, in which she leaves a parcel of pollen and nectar and lays an egg, and the nomada bee comes along and also lays an egg. This hatches into a grub, which eats the other grub and its store of pollen and nectar, and emerges the following spring to start the process all over again.

How to attract them Create the perfect conditions for ground-nesting solitary bees, such as bare patches of sandy soil and closely clipped lawns.

Red mason bee (Osmia rufa)

This solitary bee nests in old wood and hollow plant stems, even walls (although no damage is done), and readily uses bee hotels. Mason bees get their name from their habit of sealing their nests with mud. The red mason bee is said to be one of the most efficient pollinators of spring fruit trees, including apples, plums and cherries.

Covered in gingery red hairs, adults emerge from early spring onwards, and are normally on the wing until early summer. Males are smaller than females and sport a little tuft of white hair on the face. They mate, and the female lays eggs near where she was born – she may even return to the same bee hotel.

How to attract them Make a solitary bee hotel (see page 29), and leave a dish of mud out in spring, in case of dry weather.

Wasps

Wasps tend to have very little body hair and a thin waist. Most social wasps, including hornets, have yellow-and-black or yellow-and-brown striped bodies. Parasitic wasps range in colour – many are black with either orange, red or yellow markings and they often have an extremely long ovipositor (egg-laying organ).

Lifecycle Social wasps make intricate nests from chewed wood, which they rasp from untreated fence posts, fences, trees and even garden furniture. Nests can house up to 20,000 workers. Parasitic wasps lead solitary lives, laying eggs in, or near, other insects.

BELOW A common wasp takes nectar from angelica flowers. Note its thin waist and yellow legs.

Common wasp *(Vespula vulgaris)*

The common wasp is virtually hairless and is easily recognised by its bright yellow-and-black body and anchor-shaped facial mark. Like bumblebees, it lives in annual colonies, but workers feed caterpillars and other insects to the young rather than pollen and nectar, in return for a sugary substance secreted by the grubs. They only annoy us humans in late summer, when the nest breaks down and there are no longer any grubs to feed. Without the sugary returns from the young, workers look to fruit trees, jam sandwiches and fizzy drinks for a sugary fix. They can become drunk on the alcohol in fermenting fruit, which makes them clumsy, aggressive and more likely to sting. This usually lasts for a couple of weeks before they die. Only mated queens hibernate, ready to start a new generation of pest controllers the following year.

How to attract them If you can't love them, do try to tolerate them. They play a key role in the garden ecosystem and do a sterling job of keeping pests under control.

Parasitic wasps

Many wasps are solitary and parasitic, rather than living in large colonies. The most noticeable in our gardens are the ichneumons. Females often have incredibly long ovipositors, which may be mistaken for a terrifying sting. Eggs are laid in, on, or next to eggs, larvae, pupae or adults of other insects or spiders, and the emerging grub eats its host.

Some species, such as the giant ichneumon (*Rhyssa persuasoria*), locate prey deep within rotting wood. The female detects her prey by scent or from vibrations in the wood, and uses her long ovipositor to bore down and lay an egg next to her victim. The egg hatches and the grub eats its host, before overwintering, and then pupating in spring.

How to attract them Grow plenty of plants, make a log pile and tolerate caterpillars.

ABOVE *An ichneumon wasp rests on a plant stem. The long ovipositor is used to lay eggs on or near unsuspecting victims.*

Butterflies and moths

There's something about watching a beautiful butterfly visiting a beautiful flower that makes everything seem all right with the world. Who can resist the charms of the peacock, or fail to be enchanted by the common blue? Sadly, of the 440 European species of butterfly, far fewer will visit gardens, unless you live near a particularly good habitat such as a hay meadow, well-managed woodland or chalk downland. On top of that, very few can be encouraged to breed in our gardens. But, the good news is that many will stop for lunch.

Moths readily breed in gardens, although many are night flyers, so frequently go unnoticed. They're often seen as the ugly cousins of butterflies, but they can be just as beautiful and many are absolutely fascinating. Did you know that some have developed ears so they can hear bats?

OPPOSITE *A red admiral butterfly takes nectar from a willow catkin.*

HELP!

There's a butterfly in my house. Will it survive?

Most butterflies and moths overwinter as eggs, larvae or pupae, but some, including the brimstone, comma, peacock and small tortoiseshell, hibernate as adults. They need cool, dry conditions, and the small tortoiseshell and peacock will occasionally come into houses. Unfortunately, when central heating comes on in winter, the butterflies can wake up and waste energy fluttering about.

What can I do? Gently scoop it into a box and pop it in a cool, dry spot such as a shed or garage. Close the box to help the butterfly settle down if it is awake, but do remember to open it again and leave a door or window open in spring, so it can find its way outside.

Ten things to do for butterflies and moths

❶ Grow caterpillar food-plants, including nettles, buckthorn, hops and lady's smock (see page 42).

❷ Grow a variety of nectar-rich plants (see page 36) from early spring to late autumn, planting them in large, easy-to-find groups.

❸ Leave windfall apples for butterflies to drink from in autumn.

❹ Plant native deciduous trees and shrubs.

❺ Cultivate a meadow (see page 24) or patch of long grass.

❻ Plant a hedge and avoid trimming it every year (then cut it in late winter).

❼ Use rocks or large stones to create basking areas for butterflies in full sunshine.

❽ Avoid clearing ornamental borders in autumn.

❾ Tolerate a few weeds, such as bramble, plantains, dandelion and nettles (see pages 46–47).

❿ Avoid cutting down plants in autumn which might be sheltering caterpillars or harbouring pupae.

Butterflies

Butterflies are often brightly coloured, but some are mostly white and others brown. They're categorised into six families: skippers, swallowtails, whites, nymphalids, blues, coppers and hairstreaks and, finally, metalmarks (of which there's only one in Europe – the Duke of Burgundy). The ones most likely to come into your garden are in the nymphalid family. These include the peacock and small tortoiseshell.

Lifecycle Adults emerge in spring or summer, mate, lay eggs and then die. Depending on the species, a second or even third generation may emerge later in the year, which will either mate or build up fat reserves to hibernate or migrate back to southern Europe. Most species spend winter as a larva (caterpillar) or pupa (chrysalis).

Small tortoiseshell
(Aglais urticae)

With its bright orange-and-black wings edged with a row of delicate blue dots, the small tortoiseshell is easy to identify, although it's similar to the less common (and probably extinct in Britain) large tortoiseshell.

Adults hibernate in sheds and outhouses, emerging in spring to mate and lay eggs on large clumps of nettles. Their caterpillars build communal webs to shelter from predators and emerge as adults in summer. Second-generation adults are often found feeding on buddleia bushes.

Generally widespread and common, populations in the south-east of Britain have recently suffered huge declines, in part due to the arrival of a parasitic fly, *Sturmia bella*, from mainland Europe.

How to attract them If you don't have room for a large patch of nettles growing in full sun, grow plenty of late-flowering plants such as buddleia, sedums and Michaelmas daisies (*Aster novae-angliae*).

Orange-tip
(Anthocharis cardamines)

The orange-tip is mostly white, with green mottling on the undersides of its wings. Only the male has orange wing tips; the tips of the female's wings are black. Adults are seen mostly in late spring to early summer, flying along hedgerows, the edges of woodland and in gardens.

In spring, the female lays bright orange eggs singly, rather than in groups, on the flower buds of crucifers, including hedge mustard (*Alliaria petiolata*), lady's smock (*Cardamine pratensis*), honesty (*Lunaria annua*) and dame's violet (*Hesperis matronalis*). The small, green-and-white caterpillars feed on the flowers and developing seedpods, before pupating and overwintering as a chrysalis on or near the food-plant. New adults finally emerge the following spring.

How to attract them Grow nectar-rich, spring-flowering plants, especially those that they lay their eggs on (see above).

ABOVE RIGHT *Note the mottled undersides of this male orange-tip.*
ABOVE LEFT *A small tortoiseshell takes nectar from heather flowers.*
OPPOSITE ABOVE *A meadow brown takes a rest in grass, on which it may also lay eggs.* **OPPOSITE BELOW** *A peacock butterfly visits an echinacea flower.*

Peacock (*Inachis io*)

The peacock is one of the most recognisable garden butterflies, with its beautiful 'eyed' wing markings similar to the bird after which it's named.

It's one of the most long-lived butterflies – adults hibernate in garages and outhouses (they can even come into our homes), emerging to mate in spring. The female lays clusters of eggs on large sunny beds of stinging and annual nettles, and the caterpillars shelter under communal webs over the growing tips, which they strip bare before moving on to fresh growth. They pupate and emerge as the second generation of adults in summer.

In late summer adults can be seen nectaring on buddleia to build up fat reserves for hibernation. They also feed from scabious, sedum, echinacea, teasel (*Dipsacus fullonum*) and hemp agrimony (*Eupatorium cannabinum*).

How to attract them Unless you can leave a large sunny patch of nettles, you're unlikely to encourage them to breed, but by planting late-flowering nectar plants you will have a good chance of encouraging them to stop by for lunch.

Meadow brown (*Maniola jurtina*)

The meadow brown is orange and brown with a black eye spot on the tip of the forewing. It's similar to the gatekeeper, but unlike the gatekeeper it's larger, and the eye spot has one white dot, rather than two. Females are more colourful than the males. It's typically a butterfly of grassland, woodland rides and hedgerows, but it will come into gardens with patches of meadow or long grass, and will occasionally nectar on plants such as knapweeds and scabious. It's widespread and abundant, but numbers are falling due to loss of habitat.

The meadow brown hibernates as a caterpillar, which emerges in spring and fattens up on grasses before pupating and becoming an adult in summer. After mating the female lays eggs on grass, including fescues, bents and meadow grasses. Large numbers of adults may be seen flying over vegetation – even in light rain when most butterflies take shelter.

How to attract them If you have room for a mini hay meadow, complete with meadow flowers, then make one. Otherwise a patch of grass left to grow long may lure them in.

Swallowtail (*Papilio machaon*)

This large butterfly is common and widespread over much of Europe, but rare in Britain, where it has evolved into a smaller and less brightly coloured subspecies, *britannicus*.

The British swallowtail lives exclusively in the Norfolk broads and breeds only on milk parsley (*Peucedanum palustre*). By contrast, the European swallowtail is a common garden visitor and lays eggs on a variety of umbellifers, including fennel and carrots – in some instances, it's considered a pest.

Adults fly in late spring and summer. The British swallowtail has just one brood, but its European cousin has two. Initially, caterpillars are black, marked with a band of white, but eventually become bright green with narrow black bands and orange spots. The pupae are green or light brown with a dark stripe. Like all butterflies in the Papilionidae family, adults keep their wings fluttering while feeding.

How to attract them Grow a range of nectar-rich flowers for adults.

ABOVE A swallowtail shows off its swallow-like tail streamers while nectaring on red clover. RIGHT When aphids are in short supply, the speckled wood drinks nectar from plants such as heather. OPPOSITE ABOVE A red admiral rests on a bramble leaf. OPPOSITE BELOW A comma basks in the autumn sunshine.

Speckled wood (*Pararge aegeria*)

Rich chocolate brown with creamy-white patches, the speckled wood is typically found in woodland, but is now increasingly seen in gardens. Adults usually drink honeydew (a sweet substance excreted by aphids) high up in the trees, but switch to nectar in early spring and late summer, when aphids can be in short supply.

Adults breed in grass in spring, including false brome (*Brachypodium sylvaticum*), cock's-foot (*Dactylis glomerata*) and common couch (*Elytrigia repens*). There are usually at least two broods, so you may still see them on the wing in early autumn. They hibernate in grass, either as a bright green caterpillar or a chrysalis.

How to attract them Let an area of grass grow long and provide early and late sources of nectar.

Comma *(Polygonia c-album)*

The comma is a master of disguise. Its orangey-brown, raggedy wings resemble fallen leaves when resting, and its brown-and-white caterpillars look a bit like bird droppings. But it's the white, comma-shaped mark on the undersides of the wings that gives it its name.

Adults emerge from hibernation in spring, mate and lay eggs on stinging nettles. They're less fussy than other members of the nymphalid family, so will also breed on hops (*Humulus*), currants (*Ribes*), elms (*Ulmus*) and willows (*Salix*). In some parts of Europe, they use sallow (*Salix cinerea*) and birch (*Betula*). The second generation appears in summer and may produce a third generation in milder areas. Adults fatten up on a variety of nectar-rich flowers and ripe fruit, before hibernating.

How to attract them Encourage adults to breed by growing the right plants (see above).

Red admiral *(Vanessa atalanta)*

The red admiral has dark brown or black wings with red bands and white spots near the tips. Adults migrate northwards from North Africa and the Mediterranean each year. They arrive in spring, mate and lay eggs, with their offspring emerging in summer. Second-generation adults feed from plants such as buddleia and ivy (*Hedera helix*), to build up reserves for the long flight south. They also drink the juice from blackberries and windfall fruit. In milder areas, some now overwinter rather than fly south in autumn.

The red admiral breeds on nettles. Caterpillars fold the leaves together to make a tent to shelter them from predators, and can be black, greenish brown or pale yellow, depending on their size.

How to attract them If you don't have room for a large patch of nettles growing in full sun, grow plenty of late-flowering plants such as buddleia, sedums and Michaelmas daisies (*Aster novae-angliae*).

Moths

Many moths are brown and hard to identify, but some are as colourful as butterflies, especially day-flying species. Gardeners may disturb night-flying adults during the day, which tend to rest on tree bark, sheds and outhouses. They're far more numerous than butterflies – there are 13 families of larger moths, not to mention all the micro species. Common families include the Noctuids, Geometrids and hawkmoths. Of the thousands of moth species, just a tiny proportion of them are pests – including those which eat our clothes. The vast majority of them are beautiful and endearing.

Lifecycle Similar to butterflies. While most emerge in spring and summer, many don't appear until autumn and some, such as the December moth, are active in winter. When it comes to breeding, moths are less fussy than butterflies, with most laying eggs on a wide range of plants.

Silver Y *(Autographa gamma)*
Named after the silvery Y-shaped mark that appears to be painted on each forewing, this migrant moth is easy to identify. Resident in southern Europe, parts of Asia and North Africa, it migrates north in spring, sometimes reaching as far as Finland and the Arctic Circle. Some years, adults migrate in huge numbers. They arrive in the UK and northern Europe in late spring and fly south by the first frosts of autumn.

Adults fly during the day and night, regularly visiting gardens to drink from nectar-rich flowers. Several generations occur each year, with the green caterpillars eating a range of plants including garden peas (*Pisum sativum*), cabbages (*Brassica*), white or red clovers (*Trifolium*) and stinging nettles (*Urtica dioica*).

How to attract them Grow nectar-rich plants for the adults, and nettles and clover for their caterpillars. If you find any caterpillars on your pea plants, simply transfer them to a patch of nettles or clover.

Elephant hawkmoth *(Deilephila elpenor)*
This hawkmoth is one of the most exciting moths we can encourage into our gardens. All hawkmoths have spectacular caterpillars, with a spike or horn on their 'tail'. The elephant hawkmoth's caterpillars are green or brown and have enormous eye spots and a snout (like an elephant). They feed mainly on rosebay willowherb (*Epilobium angustifolium*), but also eat bedstraws (*Galium*) and garden fuchsias. Growing up to 8cm long, the caterpillars are often found on the ground in early autumn, looking to burrow into a patch of soil to pupate for winter. The bright pink and green adults emerge from late spring to mid-summer, visiting honeysuckle (*Lonicera*) and other garden plants for nectar.

How to attract them Grow a patch of rosebay willowherb, to transfer caterpillars to, from your fuchsias.

Hummingbird hawkmoth

(Macroglossum stellatarum)

This day-flying summer migrant is becoming more of a common visitor to northern Europe, probably due to climate change. It's often mistaken for a hummingbird because it hovers before flowers, beating its wings so quickly they make an audible hum. It's actually smaller than any hummingbird.

It's hairy with a dark, white-spotted abdomen, grey front wings and orange hind wings. It has a huge proboscis, with which it drinks nectar from a variety of flowering plants including buddleia, red valerian and honeysuckle.

Caterpillars feed on bedstraws (*Galium*). Adults can't survive cold winters, so they may fly south in autumn.

How to attract them You're more likely to see them the further south you live, although they have been recorded in the far north of Scotland. Grow nectar-rich plants such as honeysuckle (*Lonicera*) and red valerian (*Centranthus ruber*).

OPPOSITE ABOVE *An elephant hawkmoth shows off its stunning pink and green colours.* **OPPOSITE BELOW** *The silver 'Y' on each wing is clearly visible on this resting silver Y moth.* **BELOW** *A hummingbird hawkmoth hums and hovers, poking its huge proboscis into a verbena flower.*

Angle shades (*Phlogophora meticulosa*)

The angle shades moth is named after its unusual angled shape. It's brownish in colour, with triangular pink-and-green markings in the centre of each wing. Adults emerge in spring and fly mainly at night. They're often found resting on fences or garden foliage during the day. There are at least two broods every year; only the caterpillars overwinter, emerging in spring to pupate.

Some gardeners might not appreciate the angle shade caterpillar's habit of eating anything from aeoniums, chrysanthemums and dahlias, to basil (*Ocimum basilicum*) and pelargoniums. But don't forget that a large proportion of moth caterpillars are taken by birds and wasps, so they may not have much chance to damage your plants.

How to attract them Grow birch (*Betula*), red valerian (*Centranthus ruber*), ivy (*Hedera helix*) and oak (*Quercus*), onto which you can transfer any rogue caterpillars.

Ruby tiger (*Phragmatobia fuliginosa*)

This is a handsome moth, with a red body, velvety-brown front wings and pinkish hind wings (though colouring can vary, with northern moths having darker wings). It can be found in a variety of habitats, including gardens, and will also fly during the day.

In warmer regions adults fly and breed from mid-spring to early summer and again from late summer to early autumn, but in colder areas there's just one brood, typically in early summer. Their gorgeous 'woolly bear' caterpillars feed on a number of plants, including weeds such as ragworts, plantains, dock and dandelion (see page 46), heather (*Calluna vulgaris),* spindle (*Euonymus europaeus*) and broom (*Cytisus scoparius*). They overwinter as caterpillars in leaf litter and other debris.

How to attract them Tolerate a few weeds to grow as caterpillar food-plants, make leaf piles and avoid tidying borders in autumn for overwintering caterpillars.

ABOVE *The ruby tiger is so beautiful, it's a real treat to find one in the garden.* **LEFT** *The gorgeous triangular pink-and-green markings of the angle shades are clearly visible against the bark.* **OPPOSITE ABOVE** *A mint moth rests on catmint foliage.* **OPPOSITE BELOW** *Planting a mini-meadow is well worth doing if you end up with the six-spot burnet in your garden.*

Mint moth (*Pyrausta aurata*)

This common little moth is often found in gardens, as its larval food-plants include spearmint (*Mentha spicata*), apple mint (*Mentha rotundifolia*), marjoram (*Origanum vulgare*), lemon balm (*Melissa officinalis*) and catmint (*Nepeta*). Adults are often found resting on the leaves of mint or related species, and will fly up, and back down, if disturbed.

It typically has two generations; one in spring/early summer and another in late summer. It flies during the day and night. Caterpillars pupate and hibernate as a pupa, before emerging as an adult in spring.

How to attract them Grow plenty of its larval food-plants (although you probably already do).

Six-spot burnet (*Zygaena filipendulae*)

With its velvety-black thorax and inky wings dotted with large, scarlet blobs, the six-spot burnet is one of the most beautiful day-flying moths (well, I think so). Adults fly in summer and are usually found in flowery grassland and woodland rides, but they may come into gardens where long grass is provided. Adults are often seen nectaring on thistles (*Cirsium* and *Carduus*), knapweeds (*Centaurea*) and scabious.

There are several burnet moths, which superficially look like the mostly night-flying cinnabar, but they can be told apart from the cinnabar by their longer, chunkier antennae, narrower forewings and lack of red wing stripe. The six-spot burnet has six red spots on each forewing (most species have five). Sometimes the spots can be fused together and are occasionally yellow.

Caterpillars feed mainly on common bird's-foot trefoil (*Lotus corniculatus*) and hibernate over winter. They emerge in spring, pupate in a papery cocoon attached to grass stems, and become adults in summer.

How to attract them Plant a meadow with flowering plants such as scabious and knapweeds, and don't forget the bird's-foot trefoil.

Beetles

When it comes to garden wildlife, beetles are often overlooked. They're not nearly as popular as bees and butterflies; you don't find gardening articles entitled 'Save the beetle!', and few writers try to explain how lovely they are (except for the ladybird, which many people don't even realise is a beetle). Perhaps it's because many live in compost bins or among leaf litter, or because their grubs often look a bit like maggots (and can be garden pests). But beetles are just as interesting (and even beautiful) as bees and butterflies. Many of them are also declining.

The beetle family is the largest group of insects in the world. Beetles come in a wide variety of shapes, colours and sizes; some eat our plants, while others eat garden pests that feed on our plants. They typically have a thick pair of front wings or wing cases, called elytra, which protect the more delicate hind wings used for flying. Others don't fly at all.

Look out for beetles anywhere, from your plants to your compost bin and log pile. The larvae of many, such as chafer grubs, tend to look like maggots, but others are more attractive. Some ladybird larvae look a bit like baby crocodiles.

ABOVE *The crocodile-like larva of a ten-spot ladybird homes in on an aphid colony.* **OPPOSITE** *Pollen beetles and a balloon fly on an ox-eye daisy.*

Ten things to do for beetles

❶ Leave dead wood on trees, where possible, to provide a breeding habitat for species such as the wasp beetle.

❷ Make a log pile to provide a breeding habitat (see page 22); bury some of the logs in the ground if you can.

❸ Sweep fallen leaves under your hedge or gather in a wire cage for overwintering beetles and their prey (see page 20).

❹ Mulch borders with leaf mould, which some species may use to hunt prey.

❺ Provide a further source of dead wood by leaving an old tree stump to rot into itself.

❻ Create areas of densely planted vegetation to provide cover from predators.

❼ Plant an oak (if you have space), which many beetles will use as food and shelter.

❽ Grow a patch of nettles for aphid-eating ladybirds.

❾ Grow deciduous trees including sycamore (*Acer pseudoplatanus*). Mildew will form on the leaves, providing food for the orange ladybird.

❿ Grow a range of flowering plants, including umbellifers which may attract soldier beetles.

Two-spot ladybird (*Adalia bipunctata*)

The two-spot ladybird is smaller than the more familiar seven-spot, and has a narrower body shape. It comes in many colour forms, the two commonest being red with one black spot on each wing case, or black with two red spots on each wing case. The spots can be variable and can appear square-shaped or as splodges.

Since the arrival of the harlequin ladybird (*Harmonia axyridis*) to Europe, two-spot populations have suffered. Harlequins were first recorded in Belgium in 2001 and Britain in 2004. The two-spot ladybird has since declined by 30 per cent in Belgium and 44 per cent in Britain. The harlequin and two-spot are both tree-dwelling aphid-eaters, and it's thought that the harlequin – which is bigger, stronger and breeds more often – outcompetes the two-spot, as well as eating the larvae when aphids are in short supply.

How to attract them Avoid killing aphids and grow nettles.

Seven-spot ladybird (*Coccinella septempunctata*)

The most common and easily recognised ladybird. It has red wing cases marked with seven black dots (three on either wing case and one spread over the junction of the two).

Adults emerge in spring, mate and the female lays eggs on plants infested with aphids. When the eggs hatch, the crocodile-like larvae (see picture on page 120) hoover up the aphids, before attaching to a leaf and pupating into an orange and black pupa. The adult usually hatches out within a week. There's normally just one brood a year, with the second generation fattening up on aphids in preparation for hibernation.

How to attract them Grow nettles to attract the nettle aphid early in the year.

ABOVE LEFT *A two-spot ladybird rests on a leaf.* **ABOVE RIGHT** *A seven-spot ladybird explores an unfurling bracken stem.* **OPPOSITE LEFT** *A harlequin rests on a leaf.* **OPPOSITE RIGHT** *Revealing its appetite for aphids, this harlequin makes light work of a greenfly.*

Harlequin ladybird *(Harmonia axyridis)*

The harlequin is an alien invader of the worst kind. Originally from Asia, but introduced as biological pest control in the United States and Europe, it's been bred to be larger, stronger, faster and hungrier than its Asian ancestors. It was only a matter of time before it spread over the Channel to Britain.

It is difficult to tell apart from native species, although it tends to be bigger and has more of a domed body shape. You're likely to find one of three colour forms in your garden: red or orange with black spots (*Succinea*); black with four red spots (*Spectabilis*); and black with two red spots (*Conspicua*).

The only thing the harlequin ladybird has going for it is its appetite for aphids, but it also eats moth eggs, lacewings and other native ladybirds, such as the two-spot.

How to attract them Avoid killing them as you may kill a native ladybird by mistake. There's no chance of deterring them I'm afraid – they're here to stay!

HELP!

Why are ladybirds coming into my house?

The two-spot and harlequin are the most likely species to come into houses. They turn up in autumn looking to hibernate, and release a hormone to attract others to join them. Sometimes hundreds of ladybirds can gather in the same spot. In cool rooms they just settle down for winter and disappear again in mid-spring, but in heated rooms they don't settle and can fly around, stain furniture and even bite people. Due to being active but unable to eat as there's no food for them, many die.

What can I do? If you're happy to cohabit with them, let them get on with it, but do try to turn the heating off in the room they're sheltering in. If you'd rather they spent winter elsewhere, gather them up in a shoe box and pop them somewhere cool and dry, such as your shed or garage. Make sure they can escape in spring.

Violet ground beetle *(Carabus violaceus)*

Ground beetles are a must-have in gardens, for the simple reason that they eat snails and other garden pests. There are hundreds of different types, with the violet ground beetle being one of the easiest to identify. This is large (3cm long) and black, with a metallic violet sheen to the edges of its wing cases and thorax. Adults hunt at night, hiding by day under logs or stones. They don't fly, but they're very fast runners.

As with other beetles in the *Carabus* genus, both adults and their larvae prey on slugs, snails, worms and insects. After mating, females lay their eggs in soil. The larvae start hunting as soon as they've hatched out of the egg.

How to attract them Make a log pile and mulch your borders with leaf mould. If you find grubs in the soil, cover them up again.

Wasp beetle *(Clytus arietis)*

With its black-and-yellow banded body and relatively short antennae, this long-horn beetle pretends to be a wasp to avoid being eaten by predators. It even mimics the common wasp's jerky movements and can emit a threatening buzz when disturbed. But it doesn't sting and is completely harmless, despite its appearance.

Adults are thin and long-bodied, and fly from late spring to mid-summer. You might spot them scrambling over vegetation on sunny days. They feed on a variety of flowers for pollen and nectar, although females also eat small insects.

After mating, the female seeks out dead, rotting wood, including dead branches and even untreated garden-fence posts, to lay eggs. The larvae live and feed in this dead wood, before pupating and emerging as adults the following year.

How to attract them Ensure there is plenty of dead wood in your garden, especially if it's still attached to trees.

Common cockchafer *(Melolontha melolontha)*

Also known as the May bug, because it flies in May, the common cockchafer is large, brown and noisy. It has a black thorax, rusty-brown wing cases, brown legs and wonderful feathery antennae.

Cockchafers used to be common, but because their larvae eat plant roots, they became victims of pesticide campaigns across Europe and were almost wiped out in the 1970s. Numbers are now recovering, but they're nowhere near as common as they used to be.

Adults appear in late spring and live for up to seven weeks, feeding on flowers and leaves. During that time, they mate and the female lays eggs in the soil. The larvae feed on plant roots for several years, before eventually pupating one autumn. The cockchafer then overwinters as an adult, emerging in spring.

How to attract them Plant shrubs and trees, which groups of adults sometimes fly around.

Red soldier beetle *(Rhagonycha fulva)*

Although known as the *Weichkäfer* (soft beetle) in Germany, in Britain it's sometimes called the bonking beetle, for rather obvious reasons. If you have them in your garden, you will nearly always find them mating on flowers.

There are many types of soldier beetle, all with narrow bodies and long antennae. Up to 1cm in length, *Rhagonycha fulva* is yellow-red, with black tips on the wing cases.

OPPOSITE ABOVE LEFT *A violet ground beetle rests in tree bark.*
OPPOSITE ABOVE RIGHT *A wasp beetle strikes a sinister pose on a leaf.*
OPPOSITE BELOW *A cockshafer shows off its gorgeous feathery antennae.*

Adults fly in summer and feed on insects, which they hunt from flowers. After mating, the female lays her eggs in the soil and the brown larvae feed on small snails and insects. A year later, the larvae pupate and emerge as adult beetles.

How to attract them Plant a mini-meadow (see page 24).

Rove beetles

An enormous genus of beetles *(Ocypus)* that you may find in your compost bin. They're easy to tell apart from other beetles because their wing cases don't cover their abdomens, so they look a bit half-dressed. One of the most well recognised is the devil's coach-horse beetle (*Ocypus olens*), which is black and known for raising its abdomen like a scorpion when disturbed (it's harmless, but might give you a nip if handled).

Most rove beetles prey on insects and other invertebrates, such as snails, worms and caterpillars. Some also eat slug and snail eggs, fungus gnat larvae and aphids, so they're well worth creating habitats for in the garden! The tiny eggs are laid in groups, often close to a potential food source. The larvae then feed for a couple of weeks before pupating in soil.

How to attract them Compost waste, make log piles and mulch your plants.

BELOW LEFT *Two bonking beetles (red soldier beetles) live up to their name.*
BELOW RIGHT *A devil's coach horse beetle makes a threatening gesture.*

Flies

For many people, the word 'fly' conjures images of irritating houseflies, or rotting carrion, faeces and maggots. Then there are the mosquitoes, midges and horse flies. Surely they're not worthy of being welcomed into the garden?

And yet flies are an invaluable source of food for countless other species. Swifts, swallows, house martins and many other birds eat flies, as do bats, dragonflies and amphibians. Without flies, we wouldn't have these other species, and some, such as swifts, bats and sparrows, are already declining due to a general lack of insects, including flies!

As well as being a nutritious source of food, flies are also valuable in their own right. Many have the incredibly important job of helping to break down decaying matter, while others, such as hoverflies, eat aphids.

LEFT *A hoverfly visits a flower for pollen.* **OPPOSITE ABOVE** *A close look at a bee-fly, with its spindly legs, large eyes and rigid proboscis, reveal how different to bees it actually is.* **OPPOSITE BELOW** *As with most hoverflies, this marmalade hoverfly can be identified as male by its holoptic (fused together) eyes.*

Ten things to do for flies

❶ Grow a variety of flowering plants, particularly umbellifers such as cow parsley (*Anthriscus sylvestris*).

❷ Dig a pond or bog garden, which many flies will use to breed in (see page 56).

❸ Compost waste to provide a breeding habitat for many species (see page 18).

❹ Leave an old tree stump standing (especially if it collects water) to provide a breeding habitat for eristalis hoverflies.

❺ Let an area of grass grow long to provide shelter for crane flies and other flies.

❻ Tolerate aphids – which many hoverfly species rely on for food.

❼ Steep leaves in water to make an organic plant food, which will attract dung flies and *Eristalis* hoverflies.

❽ Make a pile of grass clippings to provide shelter and breeding habitat.

❾ Create overwintering sites by mulching borders and making leaf piles (see page 20).

❿ Grow a variety of caterpillar food-plants, for parasitic flies (see page 42).

Large bee-fly *(Bombylius major)*

If you see a large, ginger-brown, furry-looking 'bee' with an enormous proboscis visiting your primroses (*Primula*), grape hyacinths (*Muscari*), violas or bugle (*Ajuga*), it's bound to be the large bee-fly. This is not a bee, but a bee mimic, which hums and hovers and darts quickly around spring flowers. On closer inspection, you can tell it's a fly because it has only one pair of wings (bees have two). The wings are dark and the body is brown and furry, and it has a protruding rigid proboscis, which it uses to drink nectar.

After mating, the female flicks her eggs into the underground nests of solitary bees and wasps, and the larvae feed on the stores of food and grubs inside. She may also lay eggs on flowers visited by solitary bees and wasps, and the larvae hitch a ride on the bodies of unsuspecting victims.

How to attract them Grow spring-flowering plants (see above), and provide bare patches of ground for solitary bees to nest in.

Marmalade hoverfly *(Episyrphus balteatus)*

The marmalade hoverfly is a small, tiger-striped insect, which feeds on pollen and nectar from a variety of garden flowers. Males establish territories, which they guard religiously, patiently waiting for females to fly past. After mating, females lay eggs on foliage close to aphid colonies, or even on plants that are likely to be colonised by aphids.

The larvae resemble Jabba the Hutt from *Star Wars*, and worm their way around plants, piercing aphids with their mouth hooks, before sucking out their innards. One larva can eat up to 200 aphids before it pupates. They're mainly active at night, and are occasionally cannibalistic, eating smaller larvae. The pupal case resembles a pear drop sweet, and may be found stuck to the leaves of plants.

How to attract them Grow a range of flowering plants and ensure there is a plentiful supply of aphids for their larvae.

Myathropa florea

This beautiful creature is one of a number of hoverflies in the *Eristalis* tribe, which start their lives as slightly less appealing rat-tailed maggots. The bright yellow-and-black-striped adults fly from late spring to mid-autumn and feed on a variety of garden umbellifers. By contrast, their larvae eat bacteria and decaying organic matter in stagnant, waterlogged detritus, such as shallow rot holes in tree stumps, compost heaps and even drains. But don't let this put you off! The 'rat tail' is merely a breathing tube that the larva uses as a snorkel, allowing it to breathe under water.

How to attract them Grow a range of umbellifers, including cow parsley (*Anthriscus sylvestris*) and bishop's flower (*Ammi majus*) and leave tree stumps to rot. If you're really keen, you could create your own 'rot hole' in a bucket – just add water and leaves.

Volucella bombylans

This hoverfly is also a bee mimic, part of a genus of large, dramatic looking hoverflies. To the untrained eye, *Volucella bombylans* looks similar to a bumblebee, but on closer inspection it has one pair of (dark) wings.

There are several subspecies, which mimic different bumblebees. *Volucella bombylans* var. *bombylans* has an orange tail, and so mimics the red-tailed bumblebee, while *Volucella bombylans* var. *plumata* has a white tail, mimicking the white-tailed bumblebee.

Adults are found in gardens (as well as along hedgerows, in urban waste ground and woodland margins) from late spring until early autumn. They feed on nectar and pollen, and the larvae feed on the debris (and occasionally the larvae) of bumblebee and social wasp nests. Adults are often seen sunning themselves on leaves or fence posts.

How to attract them Grow a good range of flowering plants in spring and summer.

Common bluebottle (*Calliphora vomitoria*)

Bluebottles have big red eyes and a metallic-blue abdomen with black markings. They feed on nectar as well as carrion, and pollinate strong-scented flowers such as golden rod (*Solidago*). The larvae feed on faeces and carcasses of dead animals, before pupating in soil. Adults emerge after two or three weeks and are ready to mate within hours.

ABOVE *The single pair of wings and large eyes indicate that* Volucella bombylans *is a fly, not a bee.* **LEFT** Myathropa florea *basks on a leaf.*

Bluebottles might not be the most obvious species you'd want to attract to your garden, but they play an important role, helping to clear decaying matter. They're also food for spiders, amphibians, birds and bats. While it's a good idea to prevent bluebottles from landing on your food, there's no reason why they shouldn't be welcomed into your garden.

How to attract them Grow strong-scented flowers and compost waste.

Common yellow dung fly *(Scathophaga stercoraria)*

This fly is prettier than its name suggests. Adult males are golden yellow and slightly furry, while females are a little duller. They eat mainly smaller flies, but also visit flowers and may be observed waiting on flowers to hunt prey. Males also feed on blowflies (such as bluebottles) when visiting dung.

The female lays her eggs in dung and is very fussy when it comes to choosing the right spot. To prevent her eggs becoming waterlogged or drying out, she lays them on small 'hills' on the dung's surface. The eggs hatch into predatory larvae, which eat other insect larvae within the dung. They feed for up to three weeks before pupating in the soil and eventually emerge as adults.

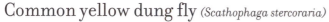

How to attract them Grow a range of nectar-rich flowers.

ABOVE LEFT *Bluebottles play an important role in the garden ecosystem.* **ABOVE RIGHT** *The squared-off end indicates this is a male.* **LEFT** *A golden-yellow dung fly.*

European or common crane fly
(Tipula paludosa)

This is one of many species of crane fly you'll find dancing around your lawn in summer and autumn. The long-legged, spider-like flies are also known as 'daddy long-legs' and are often cursed by gardeners for their leatherjacket larvae, which eat plant roots and can, in large numbers, cause unsightly brown patches in lawns.

Tipula paludosa has a slender, grey-brown body and long legs. Males have a swollen and square-ended abdomen (which I think looks like it's been wrapped in Sellotape), while the females have a pointed end, which is used to push eggs into the soil.

The larvae form an important food source for birds. It's even been suggested that the decline of starlings is the result of pesticide use, which has reduced numbers of crane flies in agricultural areas. So, if you can tolerate them in your garden, you could well help to prevent further starling declines.

How to attract them Keep areas of your lawn fairly short.

Bugs

Contrary to the belief that 'bug' is just another name for a creepy-crawly, a bug is actually an insect in the order Hemiptera, as a beetle is in the order Coleoptera. Many bugs look a lot like beetles, but they all have a straw-like sucking mouthpart called a beak or rostrum, whereas beetles have mandibles for chewing. Your garden and pond are probably full of bugs without you even noticing (take a look in the Pond life section, pages 136–139, for more bugs), but here are just two that are common and easy to recognise.

LEFT *The nymph of a green shield bug negotiates a rosemary leaf.*

Ten things to do for bugs

❶ Plant a hedge, including hawthorn (*Crataegus monogyna*), which may attract the hawthorn shield bug.

❷ Grow soft fruit, such as raspberries and blackberries. It's good to share!

❸ Grow a patch of nettles, for the nettle aphid.

❹ Grow a variety of herbaceous plants.

❺ Let a patch of grass grow long (see page 24).

❻ Make a log pile (see page 22).

❼ Sweep fallen leaves under your hedge or gather them in a bespoke wire cage (see page 20).

❽ Mulch borders with leaf mould (see page 20).

❾ Tolerate weeds, such as sorrel and dock.

❿ Grow a range of flowering plants to provide general cover, and foliage for bugs to nibble on.

Green shield bug *(Palomena prasina)*

The green shield bug is one of a number of bugs named for their shield-like shape (though they're sometimes known as 'stink bugs', owing to the marzipan-like odour they release if handled). Adults are broad, flat and green with a brown 'tail'. In autumn, they develop more subdued, browny-bronze colourings, possibly to blend in with their surroundings.

Adults feed by sucking sap from a wide range of plants, but generally don't cause any damage. They appear in spring and spend a month feeding before mating. Females lay hexagonal batches of greenish eggs on the underside of leaves. The nymphs, or baby shield bugs, which are pale green with black markings and have a more rounded shape than the adults, stay on the plant in little groups. They metamorphose into adults in time to feed themselves up prior to hibernation.

How to attract them Pack your garden with foliage.

Aphids

Aphids are the scourge of gardeners, despised for distorting plant growth and excreting a sticky substance that attracts ants and sooty mould. Yet they're some of the most important insects to have in the garden.

They suck sap from plants, piercing the stems and foliage using their beak, or rostrum. Some, such as the blackfly (*Aphis fabae*), attack a wide range of plants, while others, including the nettle aphid (*Microlophium carnosum*), eat only one plant (in this case, nettles). But look what eats them: ladybirds and their larvae, birds and their young, parasitic wasps, hoverfly larvae, lacewings. The house sparrow even depends on aphids to feed its young. So, to give aphids a home in your garden is to provide food for countless other species.

How to attract them You don't really need to do anything to attract aphids – but by tolerating them you'll provide food for a huge variety of other species.

ABOVE *A shield bug nymph rests on a kidney vetch flower.* **LEFT** *Aphids are making a meal of this rose, while a ladybird larva looks on.*

Other minibeasts

They're often called creepy-crawlies and are some of the ugliest garden inhabitants. Many are often nocturnal or hide away in the darkest corners of our gardens. Some of them are pests, others eat pests and a few are mistaken for pests, but they're also among the most important garden creatures. You don't need to go out of your way to specifically attract them – there are likely to be plenty already in your garden without you realising – but there are general ways you can encourage them (see below).

LEFT *A garden spider rests on a web suspended between thistles.*
OPPOSITE ABOVE LEFT *This female lies at the centre of her web, waiting for prey to become entangled.* **OPPOSITE ABOVE RIGHT** *An earwig shows off its tail pincers.* **OPPOSITE BELOW** *Ants patrol an aphid colony, milking the blackfly for honeydew, and warding off predators.*

Ten things to do for other minibeasts

1. Dig a pond (see page 56).
2. Compost waste (see page 18).
3. Let an area of grass grow long (see page 24).
4. Create overwintering sites by mulching borders, sweep fallen leaves under your hedge or gather them in a bespoke wire cage (see page 20).
5. Make a log pile (see page 22).
6. Grow climbers up walls and fences, to provide cover.
7. Create areas of densely planted vegetation.
8. Grow as many deciduous trees as you can.
9. Plant a hedge, as food and shelter.
10. Avoid tidying the herbaceous borders in autumn.

aphids. Adults hunt at night and hide by day.

The loveliest thing about earwigs is that the females are good mothers. They lay 20–30 eggs under stones and in crevices, which they protect from predators and gently clean. After the nymphs have hatched, their mother stays with them until they're big enough to fend for themselves.

Garden spider *(Araneus diadematus)*

The garden spider is rarely spotted outside autumn, when adults suddenly turn up in large webs spun across paths and in large shrubs.

It ranges in colour from light yellow to dark grey, but always has mottled markings across its back, with five or more large white dots forming a cross. Females are larger than males. The web is spun by the female, which usually lies head down, waiting for prey to become entangled.

The web also provides a platform on which to mate, although the male approaches cautiously. After mating, the female builds a silken sac in which to lay her eggs and then spends the rest of her life looking after them. She dies in late autumn and her spiderlings hatch out the following spring.

Common earwig *(Forficula auricularia)*

The name 'earwig' comes from the old English word 'earwicga', which means 'ear beetle', as it was once thought that they burrowed into people's ears at night to lay eggs in their brains. They're very unlikely to do such a thing!

The common earwig is small, shiny and brown, with distinctive tail pincers. It's often regarded as a pest, as it nibbles dahlia and chrysanthemum flowers, but it also eats decaying plant material, carrion and other insects, including

Black ant *(Lasius niger)*

The black ant, which is one of a number of ant species we might find in our gardens, lives in large colonies like social bees and wasps. Colonies can last for up to several years, with workers bringing food back to the nest for the grubs.

Gardeners are not generally fond of ants, as they sometimes make nests in inconvenient spots such as compost bins and plant pots, and they have an annoying habit of 'farming' aphids (the ants 'milk' the aphids for their sweet honeydew, and in exchange help to protect the aphids from predators). Sometimes they turn up in kitchen cupboards. However, they also eat caterpillars and other insects, and are themselves food for common toads, lizards and birds, including the green woodpecker, which pretty much only eats ants. On 'Flying Ants' Day', when thousands of males and daughter queens take to the sky to mate and establish new colonies, gulls, swallows and starlings have a feast.

Harvestmen (Opiliones)

Opiliones, commonly known as harvestmen, are related to spiders and look superficially like them. They don't have a clearly defined waist however, so they can be told apart from spiders by the appearance of having just one, small body. They typically have much longer legs than spiders, too.

Harvestmen don't build webs, have fangs or the ability to produce venom, and prey on a variety of invertebrates using hooks on their legs. Unlike spiders, they can chew food, and defend themselves against predators by releasing a foul smell. They can even shed a leg or two to escape.

ABOVE *The long legs of this harvestman identify it from a spider.* **BELOW LEFT** *This worm is putting itself in danger of being eaten, by travelling across grass.* **BELOW RIGHT** *A beautiful lacewing rests on a plant stem.*

Earthworms

There are lots of different types of earthworm, all of which recycle decaying matter into valuable humus. In doing so, they aerate the soil, aid drainage and make nutrients more available to plants. They're also food for hedgehogs, badgers, birds and amphibians.

Earthworms live in a variety of habitats, depending on the species. The thin, reddish brandling worm (*Eisenia fetida*) is found in large numbers in compost heaps and leaf piles, while larger, pinker worms, such as the garden earthworm (*Lumbricus terrestris*) live beneath lawns and borders. If you go out at night with a torch, you might catch a glimpse of leaves being pulled beneath the soil surface by worms.

Worms are hermaphrodite. Breeding takes place in summer with an exchange of sperm, then each worm lays a cocoon of eggs in the soil.

Common green lacewing (*Chrysoperla carnea*)

The common green lacewing is a pretty little thing, lime green with copper eyes and delicate, translucent, lacy wings. The brown and stripy larvae are far less attractive, but they make up for this by eating huge numbers of aphids. They have enormous mandibles (jaws), which they use to grasp their prey in order to suck out their innards. (Adults also eat aphids but not as many, and they may also drink nectar.)

Lacewings are not true flies, and belong to the order Neuroptera. There are many different species of green and brown lacewing, some of which are rare or threatened.

You may come across adults at rest on a tree branch or plant stem. The female lays her eggs in groups, placing each one on a thread of

mucus, which she attaches to a leaf. The mucus hardens in the air and each egg is left suspended on a stalk, resembling a collection of drop earrings.

Adults hibernate over winter, often coming into homes, sheds or greenhouses. They turn pinkish-brown at this time, possibly to blend in better with their surroundings.

Woodlice, centipedes and millipedes

If you lift a log in your garden, you're likely to find centipedes, millipedes and woodlice, which will quickly run to shelter. Although rarely seen, they play an important role in gardens, and are not pests.

Woodlice are found in compost heaps and rotting wood, and are sometimes blamed for damage to strawberry crops (which is more likely to have been the work of slugs). They're actually crustaceans and are distantly related to crabs and other sea creatures, but have evolved to survive life on land. There are several species likely to come into our gardens, some of which may roll into a ball when threatened. They eat decaying organic matter, including dead leaves, and they're eaten by spiders, shrews, toads and some birds.

Centipedes are voracious carnivores, which feed on spiders, worms, woodlice, caterpillars and snails. Millipedes, which sometimes look like woodlice, eat decaying plant matter.

ABOVE FROM LEFT *Woodlouse, centipede and millipede, which all look similar and shelter together, but have different roles in the garden.*

Pond life

One of the best things about having a pond is the variety of wildlife you'll attract. As well as amphibians and the odd reptile, you'll find countless other creatures inhabiting the watery world beneath the surface. These all have a vital role to play, not least in providing a source of food for amphibians, birds and bats. Many of them, such as dragonflies and damselflies, are themselves predators of smaller larvae, including tadpoles. It's a tough life, being pond life.

LEFT *A blue-tailed damselfly rests on a blade of grass, beside a pond.*

Ten things to do for pond life

❶ Dig a pond (as large as you have space for) with gentle sloping sides (see page 56).

❷ Grow lots of aquatic vegetation to provide shelter for aquatic larvae.

❸ Avoid adding fish to your pond, which can eat a lot of aquatic invertebrates.

❹ Add a log or two to your pond.

❺ Create habitats for flies in the garden, for dragonflies and damselflies to eat.

❻ If you need to clear your pond, do so in autumn, to cause the least disturbance to pond life.

❼ Create basking sites in your garden, using rocks or large stones.

❽ Add sticks or grow tall, emergent marginal plants to act as perches for damselflies and dragonflies.

❾ Remove large amounts of blanketweed from your pond by hand, as this can block light.

❿ Avoid topping up the pond with tap water.

Dragonflies and damselflies

These magnificent creatures have barely changed in 300 million years, which is a good thing as they're incredibly lovely. Dragonflies are bigger and more robust-looking than damselflies. They're often found away from water and rest with their wings at right angles, like old-fashioned fighter planes. Damselflies are more slender and dainty, are rarely found away from water and rest with their wings shut.

Lifecycle Both dragonflies and damselflies breed in water, such as ponds, but some prefer canals, rivers and peat bogs. The larvae are predatory, feeding on a variety of aquatic larvae such as mosquito and midge larvae, aquatic worms, and occasionally small tadpoles and fish. Again, damselfly larvae are more slender and delicate than their cousins.

Common darter *(Sympetrum striolatum)*

If you have dragonflies visiting your garden pond, you'll almost certainly see the common darter. The orange-red males are easier to spot, while females are more of a yellow-brown colour. You may see territorial males perched in prominent positions from which they can dart after intruders, before returning to exactly the same spot.

Like all dragonflies, the common darter eats a variety of insects, including mosquitoes, midges, small moths and flies. As it moves closer to its prey, it uses its front legs to form a 'basket', to scoop up its quarry. But it always returns to its perch to eat.

Mating takes place near water and egg-laying is a double-act, with the male pushing the female downwards so that her abdomen breaks the water's surface.

How to attract them Dig a pond and plant it with a variety of submerged and marginal plants.

ABOVE *A male red darter rests with his wings outstretched.*

Water boatmen and pond skaters

These bugs are often the first to colonise a new pond – you might spot them flying in on warm summer days. Many are predatory, eating a variety of insects and their larvae. Water boatmen in the genus *Corixa* spend most of their time at the bottom of the pond and are herbivores.

Lifecycle Mating takes place between early winter and late spring and eggs are laid singly among the stems of water plants. The nymphs take just two months to become adults. Male water boatmen are said to have the loudest mating calls in the world for their size; they achieve it by rubbing their penis against the abdomen.

LEFT *A male and female make the next generation of azure damselflies.* **BELOW** *It's not called a backswimmer for nothing.* **OPPOSITE** *Skating on the water's surface is no problem for pond skaters.*

Azure damselfly *(Coenagrion puella)*

Blue damselflies are hard to tell apart, but it can be done, with patience. Identifying the azure blue from the common blue depends on observing the markings on the second abdominal segment – male azures have a flat-bottomed U shape here.

The azure flies from late spring to early autumn. Males are almost electric blue, with a variety of black markings, while females are either blue or green. Mating takes place in summer and eggs are laid on aquatic plants just below the water's surface.

How to attract them Dig a pond – the larger the better – in a sunny spot in the garden. Plant it with a variety of submerged and marginal plants to provide the best possible shelter for the larvae.

Backswimmer (*Notonecta glauca*)

Also known as the greater water boatman, the backswimmer is a true bug that resembles a boat with a large pair of oars (these are actually its hind legs). Unlike the lesser water boatman, which swims on its front, the backswimmer swims on its back just under the pond's surface, trapping air under the water using its wings and hairy body.

Despite its amusing appearance, this water bug is actually a dangerous predator. Adults seek out tadpoles and water beetle larvae using their large eyes, and detect vibrations made by drowning insects as they fall in with the many hairs on their bodies. Mating takes place between early winter and late spring, and eggs are laid singly among the stems of water plants. The nymphs take just two months to become adults.

How to attract them Dig a pond with lots of shallow margins and submerged plants.

Common pond skater (*Gerris lacustris*)

The common pond skater has a thin, brownish-grey body and a small head with large eyes. It has three pairs of legs, each with its own function: the first pair is used for grasping prey, the middle pair propels it along the water surface with either a rowing or jumping motion, and the hind pair acts as rudders. Like the backswimmer, the pond skater is also covered in tiny sensitive hairs, which detect vibrations from struggling insects on the pond's surface.

Adults emerge from hibernation in mid- to late spring and mating takes place almost immediately. The second generation emerges about a month later. Between late autumn and mid-spring, pond skaters leave the pond to hibernate. They sometimes do this in groups, often taking shelter in garden sheds or outhouses.

How to attract them Dig a pond with lots of shallow margins and submerged plants.

Index

Resources

If you find a sick or injured animal you can find detailed information on how to look after it, or locate the nearest group or carer that can take it in, from the list of organisations below. You can also find up-to-date information on species identification, creating habitats, conducting surveys and activities for children. Many of these organisations are charities and rely on donations from the public – why not join one and get involved with your local group? You can make a huge difference, doing anything from buying Christmas cards to conducting bee walks or helping toads cross roads to access their mating grounds in spring. You could even learn to become a carer.

WILDLIFE CONSERVATION GROUPS

Amphibian and Reptile Groups of the UK
arguk.org

Bat Conservation Trust
bats.org.uk

British Dragonfly Society
british-dragonflies.org.uk

British Hedgehog Preservation Society (BHPS)
britishhedgehogs.org.uk

British Trust for Ornithology (BTO)
bto.org

Buglife
buglife.org.uk

Bumblebee Conservation Trust
bumblebeeconservation.org

Froglife
froglife.org

Hawk and Owl Trust
hawkandowl.org

The Mammal Society
mammal.org.uk

Moths Count
mothscount.org

Red Squirrel Survival Trust
rsst.org.uk

RSPB
rspb.org.uk

Swift Conservation
swift-conservation.org

UK Ladybird Survey
ladybird-survey.org

The Wildlife Trusts
wildlifetrusts.org

WILDLIFE GARDENING SUPPLIERS

ChapelWood Wildlife Care
chapelwoodwildlife.co.uk

Chiltern Seeds
chilternseeds.co.uk

Emorsgate Seeds
wildseed.co.uk

Habitat Aid
habitataid.co.uk

Puddleplants
puddleplants.co.uk

Really Wild Flowers
reallywildflowers.co.uk

RSPB Shop
shopping.rspb.org.uk

Wiggly Wigglers
wigglywigglers.co.uk

OTHER USEFUL RESOURCES

Bees, Wasps & Ants Recording Society
bwars.com

Field Studies Council (FSC)
field-studies-council.org

Flora Locale
floralocale.org

Natural England
naturalengland.org.uk

Royal Horticultural Society (RHS)
rhs.org.uk

Wild About Gardens
wildaboutgardens.org.uk

WWF UK
wwf.org.uk

FIELD GUIDES AND OTHER BOOKS

Bat Detective: A Field Guide for Bat Detection, Brian Briggs and David King (Batbox Ltd., 1998)

The Birdwatcher's Pocket Field Guide to Birds of Parks and Gardens, Mark Golley (New Holland Publishers Ltd., 2004)

British Moths and Butterflies, Chris Manley (A&C Black Publishers Ltd., 2008)

Field Guide to the Bumblebees of Great Britain and Ireland, Mike Edwards and Martin Jenner (Ocelli Ltd., 2009)

Garden Creepy-Crawlies, Michael Chinery (Whittet Books Ltd., 1986)

Frogs and Toads, Trevor JC Beebee (Whittet Books Ltd., 1997)

Ladybirds, Peter Kearns and M.E.N Majerus (Richmond Publishing Co. Ltd., 1989)

Mammals of the British Isles: Handbook, Stephen Harris and Derek Yalden (Mammal Society, 2008)

Pond Life, Trevor Beebee (Whittet Books Ltd., 1992)

Acknowledgements

I couldn't have written this book without the enormous support of my family, not least Mum for letting me dig her a second pond and Dad for reading vast chunks of copy. Special thanks also to Chris for letting me use her garden as a prop and doing the very important job of being lighting director, Ceals for cooking nourishing dinners and Ellie and Anna for providing alternative conversation ('I don't even know what a newt looks like').

Thank you to Euan and Pippa at AM Heath, and Emma, Jenny, Judith, Laura and Megan at Kyle Books.

Many thanks to Lawrence Arnold for one of the best days of the year at the London Wetland Centre – the smell of grass snake musk will always remind me of your kindness and generosity. We also had a fabulous morning photographing Toady in the garden of Ray and Barbara Cranfield and Alfie the hedgehog at Sue Kidger's. Thank you to Miles King for reassuring me that ragwort should be included in my list of top ten weeds and Abigail, Frances and Eden for letting me pimp their garden shed. Thanks to Debra for use of your garden for photography.

Thank you to the RSPB shop and ChapleWood for generously providing bird food and feeders for shoots, Puddleplants for supplying pond plants and baskets, and Sedum Green Roof for donating sedum plug plants. Thank you to Lorraine and Nigel from number 33 for giving me a few logs for my log pile project and @DayMoonRoseDawn for the clever idea of using flower-arranger's foam to make solitary bee habitats. The RSPB was very generous in allowing me to use their bird box plan.

I would also like to thank the experts who read through my content, in no particular order: Richard Comont, Jules Howard, Mike Toms, Fay Vass, Shirley Thompson, Richard Fox, Les Hill, Ben Darvill, Marina Pacheco and Sam Taylor and the Froglife team. You are so talented and knowledgeable and my book would be poorer without you. Thank you also to the brains of Twitter and Ispot for helping to identify various creatures.

For general support, chats and beer, I'd like to thank Janice Hardy, Eli Davis, Daniel Haynes, Andrew Macguire and Jane Powers. Thanks to Grace and Emma for turning up with a goat's cheese tartlet two days before deadline – I probably wouldn't have eaten that day if you hadn't.

Last, but by no means least, I would like to thank Julie. For standing in the rain, helping with DIY projects, taking beautiful photos, reading copy, being there when it all got too much and reminding me why I was doing this while finding it all a bit much herself. Life would be a struggle without her.